Praise for *Judg*

"Mailander deconstructs the subtle, yet powerful decision-making variables that profoundly impact a leader's success, defining how to navigate the arduous path to critical decisions, and the strategies for communicating these decisions to a company's most important stakeholders. The strategies set forth in *Judgment* create significant advantages for those companies seeking to compete at the highest level."

—Mike Doyle, President & Global CEO, Ketchum

"*Judgment* is this moment's essential read for every business and thought leader who aims to seize fast-moving opportunities, make smarter decisions under pressure, and give themselves a competitive advantage. With a profound understanding of human behavior, Chris' thought-provoking analysis cuts through the noise to shine a light on the decision dynamics that are at play in every high-stakes moment. I wholeheartedly recommend *Judgment* to anyone seeking to enhance their decision-making skills and gain a sense of clarity in today's hyper-disrupted world. Whether you are an entrepreneur or at the helm of a large organization, this book serves as the blueprint to unlocking not only your potential — but also that of your team, your organization, and your mission."

—Angelique Rewers, Founder and CEO, BoldHaus

"In this extraordinary resource for global leaders developing the strategies to tackle our greatest challenges, Mailander provides the tools and methods for curating the long arc of decision-making necessary to take on our most significant societal, economic, and climate-related challenges. *Judgment* is critical reading for global thinkers and change agents."

—Andrew Jones, Executive Director, Climate Interactive

"*Judgment* is equal parts a thrilling, suspense-filled tale of high stakes decision-making, and a sophisticated deconstruction of who won, who lost, and the lessons learned in those crucible moments."

—Robbie Bach, Former President and Chief Xbox Officer, Microsoft

"Classic Chris – his penchant for captivating storytelling is at its height in *Judgment: The Art of Momentous Decision-Making*. Aspiring and established leaders, across all walks of life, will profit from the combination of Mailander's worldly professional experience and perspective."

—Jonathan Smith, Managing Director, Fairmount Partners

"In *Judgment*, you learn how to make exceptional decisions under high pressure. This is essential reading for CEOs."

—Scott Bauer, Partner, PwC

"In *Judgment: The Art of Momentous Decision-Making*, Chris Mailander disentangles the myriad forces, inflection points, and decisions that shape the trajectory of events that lead to crucible moments. Drawing from three pivotal events—each described in vivid detail—Mailander explores how the decisions the principal actors made along the arc leading to those moments helped determine whether the players could forge successful outcomes when the stakes were at their highest. *Judgment* provides valuable insights into how to anticipate, prepare for, and make sound decisions during critical moments we will all face in our careers and lives."

—Nathan Vitan, Chief Legal Officer, Public Storage

"*Judgment* is for rising CEOs building phenomenal companies. It is for those asking how they can do more, how they can do better, and how to get it right in their critical moments. *Judgment* is for those CEOs that seek out those exceptional moments when they will be called upon to be extraordinary."

**—Chris Whitney, CEO, Whitney Logistics &
Miles Ahead Brands**

"*Judgment: The Art of Momentous Decision-Making* is an indispensable guide for those seeking to enhance their leadership capabilities, refine their decision-making acumen and embrace the extraordinary."

—Jonathan Bowman, Certified EOS Implementer®

"Chris Mailander ushers readers into the very rooms where decisions are being made, revealing the tensions and triumphs that underpin decisive moments in history. His vivid storytelling lets us experience these moments in real-time, while not skimping on the analysis, granting unique insight into the complexities of leadership during what he terms 'crucible moments'. This is more than a CEO field guide; it's a journey into the nexus of action and consequence in high-stakes environments. A truly immersive and enlightening read."

—Eliot Puplett, CEO & Co Founder of The Medici Project

"*Judgment* provides modern strategies for growing, competing, and winning, all of which are rooted in how we make the critical decisions in business and life."

—Nick Friedman, Co-Founder, College Hunks Hauling Junk

"The lessons in *Judgment* transcend leadership, regardless of company size, geography, or industry. It plucks out the deeper codes of judgment that are essential to great decision-making."

—**Derrick Raymond, Strategy & Corporate Development Leader**

"*Judgment* is for anyone making decisions that have a global impact."

—**Ann M. Steingraeber, Senior Lawyer, Cargill**

"*Judgment: The Art of Momentous Decision-Making* is a captivating exploration of the art and science behind effective decision-making. Chris Mailander skillfully presents a wide range of strategies that empower leaders to make sound and impactful decisions while steering clear of avoidable mistakes. *Judgment* is perfect for aspiring leaders, seasoned executives, and anyone seeking to enhance their decision-making capabilities."

—**Michael Morales, Chief Executive Officer, RF-SMART**

"*Judgment* sets forth the strategies enabling a high-potential company to achieve its most audacious goals."

—**Joseph McMillin, Founder and Former CEO, Atlas Organics**

"*Judgment* is filled with secrets that can help you during your most challenging and impactful moments."

—**Chris Larsen, Founder, Next Level Income**

STRATEGY & DECISIONS

JUDGMENT

THE ART
of
MOMENTOUS
DECISION-MAKING

Lessons for Leaders Drawn from
Three Crucible Moments in History

CHRIS MAILANDER

Ironheart Publishing

Hardcover: 979-8-9879639-0-6
Paperback: 979-8-9879639-1-3
eBook: 979-8-9879639-2-0

Book design by Mayfly Design

Library of Congress Catalog Number: 2023904210

To my father (1937–2022),
who spent a lifetime
deciphering the subtle clues
separating the ordinary from the extraordinary.

Who Should Read This Book

Judgment: The Art of Momentous Decision-Making
is for strategists, planners, and leaders in
the corporate boardroom, on the battlefield,
or in government.

It is for those preparing their own judgment
for when it will matter the most.

Purpose of This Book

Judgment explores real leaders
making tough decisions
under difficult circumstances.

You will see what the leaders
saw in those moments.
You will feel what they felt.
You will share their struggles
and their fears.

You, too, will face tough decisions.
They will be made under difficult circumstances.

The purpose of *Judgment* is
to build upon their experiences.

It is to prepare you
for your own crucible moments.

Contents

Preface

In the summer of 1993, a day or two after taking the bar exam, I loaded my meager belongings into the back of a farm truck I had borrowed from my father. My own car had been stolen several nights before the most important and difficult exam up to that point in my life while I studied in a downtown law library. It surfaced several days later, resting on cinder blocks just outside the gates of a Chula Vista chop shop. It had been stripped of its Chevy 305 engine and wheels. No one had apparently seen anything. The police yawned.

It was the end of my first stint in California; I was headed east. I felt a bit ashamed to admit it, but I had grown bored by San Diego's idyllic weather and vacuous conversations. I was desperate for drama and a feeling of purpose. On the long journey to the other coast, I would treat myself to a poor man's vacation. In the coming days, I would absorb the divine lands and skies of the West, infusing their grandeur and subtlety into my being. At night, I'd dream of the adventures of a life ahead.

I was down to my last $800 of borrowed money to pay for school. I pushed the old farm truck hard up the I-5 to Sacramento, then bore east on I-80 through Donner Pass, across the top of Nevada and Utah until the expanse of the Great Salt Lake opened before me, then pushed even farther until crossing into western Wyoming. It took a full day and nearly a full night. The push was necessary. It was both a physical and an emotional journey. I had to pass from one realm to the next.

The next morning, I found myself in the early light somewhere in the great expanse of Wyoming, parked along a lonely road, sleeping across the bench seat of the farm truck mounted with a wooden livestock rack and filled with my only possessions. A single coyote poked up from a ditch and sauntered briskly across the road, moving with calm and purpose. A third of my journey to the East was complete. After clearing the blur from my eyes, I set out again, making my way slowly toward the beauty of western Nebraska's rolling sand hills.

A week later, after a stop to see family living among the cornfields of Iowa, now wearing a blue suit and silk tie, I walked into an office on Connecticut Avenue in Washington, DC. They assigned me a desk on the fourth floor overlooking the steps of the Cathedral of St. Matthew the Apostle, where just three months short of thirty years earlier, little John F. Kennedy Jr. had saluted the coffin of his father, the assassinated president.

I had worked for this firm the previous summer, and they had offered me a job to return to when I finished law school. Last week's journey was now but the intermission between the realms, from student to lawyer, from West Coast to East, from one who could only imagine how power, influence, and values shaped momentous decisions to one who worked the knobs and levers to make them so. I had seemingly passed through a portal.

The firm was new, still finding its way. One of its founders had a knack for saying just the right thing at just the right moment. In a town where doors are unlocked by subtle shifts in narratives and perceptions, it was his gift. The other founder, Peter D. Robinson, was a quieter man. He could be found with his back to the door in a leather-bound swivel chair, staring out the windows into nothingness. He contemplated the arcs in the political and policy debates around town the way I imagined a conductor sees music. He felt the highs and lows amid the cacophony, saw the shapes of colors emerge from a swirling ether of grays, divined when to move forward in the debates, when to hold, and when to hide. He was a thinker and a feeler, an intellectual, and an empath. He became my mentor.

To most, political Washington is the pinnacle of chaos and dysfunction. It is messy and loud, and many of the most visible actors in two and a half centuries of ever-running theater are flawed human beings we find distasteful at best and repugnant at worst. The fundamental institution of Washington, however, endures. It has survived the stuttering steps of a young nation emerging from revolution. It has withstood civil war. It found power by emerging victorious from two world wars and then searched the depth of its soul in the wars that followed, challenging the assumptions in the country's own narrative surrounding its identity, power, and purpose. It has struggled with a recurring cycle of violent torment, torn from within, socially and culturally. It has overcome economic cataclysm, again and again. Through it all, it endures.

Something deeper, something with roots in its very DNA, grounds the country with its admirable ethos. Political Washington was conceived to withstand the worst of human behaviors with collective resolve to serve higher, more enlightened values, they being woven into the fabric of the Constitution. The system is designed to survive the messiness of change, radicalized voices, charismatic ideologues, and charlatans. It is designed to evolve and grow, all in service to ideals rooted in certain truths "self-evident." It endures also because of those silent stewards who toil not in service to their own egos or their self-selected tribes among the many, but in service to these higher ideals.

Robinson was one such steward of the ideals. He had been

a parliamentarian in the US House of Representatives, quietly managing the processes, procedures, and structures for those momentous decisions that must be made under seemingly the worst of conditions. After thirteen years in the well of the House, handing instructions to and whispering into the ear of the chair presiding over each proceeding on the floor, making sure the debates were fair and in service to the elected majority, whichever party that may be during any two-year cycle, Robinson moved to the Democratic Steering and Policy Committee. There, he spent five years advising the House leadership on how and when to introduce major pieces of legislation.

Robinson's job, in short, was to identify where wins could be achieved and how to achieve them while avoiding the bloody battles and skirmishes that waste the power that must be mustered when the nation faces crisis or opportunity. By the time my path crossed Robinson's, he possessed nearly two decades of experience in managing the processes by which Congress made decisions on the most important issues affecting Americans; their political, economic, and social institutions; and their place in the world. His realm was governed by the mysterious but practiced art of exercising judgment in critical moments of decision-making.

The young firm Robinson cofounded, and that I was now working for, had recently been acquired by a global communications company. The marriage immediately bestowed the firm with a marquee roster of clients. Within weeks, I went from sleeping in the cab of an old farm truck with only a few dollars in my pocket to advising CEOs of multinational banks, global financial institutions, credit card companies, insurers, and pharmaceutical companies. It was a gift.

Our purpose was to sort the signal from the noise of Washington's cacophony, sensing the more subtle clues that affect narratives, perceptions, timing, and the shifts in power in political Washington. It was a period during which the North American Free Trade Agreement was passed and President Bill Clinton's health care reform failed.

In this new realm, I discovered my education had only just begun. It was a crash course in judgment—the art of knowing when to move, when to fight, when to be silent, whom to trust and whom to not, how to overcome dissent, and when to become the dissenter. Our purpose was to find pathways through murky and treacherous portals to achieve something better on the other side. Robinson taught me to look for the subtle clues that would write history's next story and how to shape it.

One lesson rose above all others:

How we exercise judgment is the most powerful variable in determining whether a momentous decision leads to success or failure.

Over three decades of working with politicians, international leaders, and corporate executives, sparked by a unique launch point to a career, I've studied the alchemy of how people exercise judgment during a myriad of critical moments. It is a career that has hopped from designing award-winning public affairs campaigns for a global communications firm for the likes of Bank of Montreal, the Federal Home Loan Bank System, and Visa; to lobbying senators and members of Congress for Mastercard, Unisys, and a Blue Cross insurance company; to teaching young international lawyers at Georgetown Law School how to navigate the challenges before them; to advising on shifting landscapes in global finance and banking as an adjunct fellow at one of the preeminent foreign-policy think tanks in the world, the Center for Strategic & International Studies; to launching new technology businesses for the global systems integration arm of KPMG, subsequently spun out as part of a $3 billion initial public offering; to developing the antifraud program for the president of Nigeria and the country's massive oil sector; to managing the first-ever sale of spectrum for the Government of Iraq; to negotiating acquisitions in over forty countries in the United States, Europe, Asia, the Middle East, and Africa during both conflict and post-conflict economies; to leading a Silicon Valley tech company through its spin-out, capitalization, and growth; to advising young CEOs on unlocking the exponential value harbored within their private equity-backed companies and achieve their greatest potential. In each of these wildly diverse experiences, the essence of the challenge has been the same:

Manage a decision arc through an arduous path;
Cut through the noise and distractions to find clarity;
Shape the direction of the arc;
Shift the rules of the game;
Avoid the pitfalls;
Gain opportunity and advantage; and
Create something bold.

In the course of this journey, I've witnessed many leaders who exercised judgment brilliantly in their crucible moment. Many more did not. *Judgment* is an exploration of those deeper codes and common patterns that explain why.

Before undertaking this exploration of the underlying codes and patterns that help define where success lies, there are several precursors to understand:

Judgment itself is the product of how we have
arrived at this moment, what we do in this moment,
and whether we possess the discipline and insights to
get the critical decision right when it matters most.

Judgment is dependent on how leaders perceive, react, and think in these moments when the noise, pressure, and stakes are at their highest.

Judgment is a construct that feels familiar and readily known to all of us. As we deconstruct it to discover its more fundamental tenets, however, it becomes more mysterious. The properties of judgment have an alchemical quality to them, able to transform adversity into opportunity for gifted leaders while proving elusive, career-ending, or even fatal to others.

The unfortunate reality is that we measure judgment best only when it has failed. It is in this moment, looking backward, when we are privy to the costs of judgment poorly exercised. The more significant opportunity, however—and the place where the beholder can create advantage—is to learn those codes, methods, and techniques that enable the careful curation of judgment.

Foreword

We had to decide how to depart. It was night. The weather was not optimal. Tracer rounds pierced through the dark with gunshot reports all around us. Our airfield was situated in the lowest part of the valley. The enemy lurked somewhere above us, watching. Aircraft coming in and going out were suffering damage from small arms fire. Ground control was not helpful to the next decision. It would be a judgment call, and ours alone. We decided to depart "dirty", with flaps down, accelerating into the night at maximum power, and with no lights on the aircraft. We would leave as soon as there was a lull in the gunfire. It was a priority mission. There could be no delay. There could be no failure.

My co-pilot and I were trained for moments like this. Our training took over. Power to climb, rotate early, gear, flaps, radios. We would ascend into the night, desperate to soar through 10,000 feet, where we would finally be out of range for their guns and anti-aircraft weapons. There was a method to it. Landing at the reposture location would be another story. The air controller had nominal English. We would be on our own again, this time landing with only our instruments as the guide. Moments like this became our routine rather than the exception.

I later was stationed at the Pentagon. Decision-making here was different. It was bigger, more complex, and with more layers. I became the briefer to the senior-most leaders of the US Army before and during the invasion of Iraq, and would continue in this role during the follow-on occupation. I along with a team of nearly forty Army officers prepared the daily decision machinery by arming the command with as much operational information as possible. It was essential to their exercise of judgment in wartime.

There was a method to this as well, albeit very different. We would build tomorrow's brief the night before. I would compile, read, re-read, and absorb everything I could prior to presenting the current fact pattern to the command at an oh-dark-thirty meeting every morning. These morning briefings were dense. They covered everything from the movement and actions of the smallest Special Operations unit; to materiel transit times; to health concerns of a disease-borne pesky local sand fly (leishmaniasis); to, unfortunately, the names, hometowns and next of kin of those US service members killed in action the day before. The leaders wanted to know everything they could. It required the ability to process an absolutely herculean amount of information. What we included or did not include in the briefing, and how we shaped and presented the fact pattern, could have immeasurable impact on our success at the highest levels of military decision-making.

From the Pentagon, I became a lawyer. In my tenure within the office of the Attorney General, decision-making was again quite different. It involved different rules, different processes and a different kind of judgment than required of two pilots sitting on a darkened airfield under fire or within the immense enterprise that is the Pentagon. Here, the decision focused on the likelihood of recidivism by convicted offenders. Our job was to prepare a recommendation, based upon our judgment, for how likely it was that an offender might repeat their criminal actions. The statutory guidelines were tough. The punishments could be harsh. Sometimes rehabilitation worked. Sometimes it did not. Our job was to provide an assessment of what was most likely to happen next. It was all judgment. It was personal. It affected lives.

Yet as different as each of these situations have been, there is a common thread that pulls through each. Whether I was forcing our aircraft to climb out of hostile territory, preparing to arm senior leaders sending Americans into battle, or as a lawyer likely shaping the fate of an offender, the decision in each case turned on how we exercised judgment in a critical moment. The exercise of judgment is always, unfortunately, imperfect. The pressure is always intense. There is never enough time. The stakes are inevitably high. The risks—to oneself and for others—are very real. It is our obligation as leaders, however, to strive for the highest levels of performance.

There are ways in which our own judgment can be heightened so that the decisions we make change the arc, capture the opportunity, avoid the tragedies, and even save lives. With *Judgment: The Art of Momentous Decision-Making*, Chris Mailander has set forth the structures and methods for doing just this. He plots each point along an unfolding decision arc, highlighting what to look for and what to avoid, identifying the common errors and missteps made by leaders in crucible moments, and setting forth the lessons, rules, and tools we all can use along the way.

There is something deeper going on in Mailander's study of judgment. There are what he describes as the deeper codes and common patterns that underpin judgment in crucible moments. They are the sort of essential lessons leaders should not only understand, but operationalize within their own decision-making, whether they be young pilots on the battlefield or seasoned executives in the boardroom. What Mailander has delivered is a treatise for how to get it right when it matters most.

Colonel William P. Schwab, Esq., US Army, Retired
Current, Deputy for Combined and Joint Military Exercises
USINDO-Pacific Command
Honolulu, Hawaii
March 2023

The Experiment

 J *udgment: The Art of Momentous Decision-Making* is based upon an experiment. In this work, we will examine three case studies. They are:

Nuclear Brinkmanship in the Cold War, 1986

In the waters somewhere off the coast of Vladivostok, Russia, we study the command of the USS *Guardfish*, one of the US Navy's top weapons in the hunt for Soviet secrets. It is 1986, and the Soviet Union and the United States are locked in an escalating battle defined by political and military brinkmanship. Each of their respective gambits runs the risk of triggering nuclear annihilation. The moment-by-moment decisions made by the captain of the USS *Guardfish* and its crew deep below the darkened seas tell us much about preparing for crucible moments.

The Precipice of Global Economic Collapse, 2008

In 2008, the global economy teeters on the precipice of cataclysmic disaster. The core of the global financial system is melting down. Leading financial institutions are falling. One institution, however, is too big to let fail. If it implodes, it will take the entirety of the financial system and possibly the whole economy with it. Over the course of several days, the fate of the global financial system is determined by several dozen men in tense negotiations in quiet conference rooms across several blocks of Wall Street. The quickly shifting balance of power among them, affecting their leverage over one another and their susceptibility to events outside of their control, informs our own responses to those events we can and cannot control.

Crescendo in the Global War on Terror, 2015

Just before the world's leaders convene in Paris, seeking to attain the most significant multilateral commitments ever on global climate change, terrorists launch coordinated attacks across the city. Over the course of four hours, as friends and lovers dine in tiny bistros and fans cheer on their national soccer team taking on the world champion German opponent, France witnesses the greatest atrocity on its soil since World War II. We study the decisions made moment by moment in France, as well as from inside the White House Situation Room, the epicenter from which the United States' own national security apparatus stands up to defend against its newest threat. The events reveal lessons in responding to quickly changing conditions and formulating rational responses to fear-inducing circumstances.

Commonalities

In some ways, these case studies are similar:

- Each is historically significant;
- In each, the stakes are extremely high; and

- The pressure on the decision makers is immense. The level of uncertainty about the future that will unfold as a consequence of their decisions or indecision is at its greatest. The arc of history will change with the decisions they make or fail to make.

In each instance, I have talked with individuals at or near the center of the storm, reacting to or causing it, playing roles instrumental to shaping the decisions required in the very present moment. Again, there are commonalities in their experiences:

- The decisions required the height of their intellectual capabilities;
- They invoked the emotional body; and
- Their decisions and the resulting acts affected them in ways both consciously known and subconsciously perceived, and most likely affected their loved ones, their teams, and potentially the lives of millions of others wholly unaware of the catastrophic possibilities ahead.

As such, given the gravity of the moment, the individual's very being is affected. Their altered being affects their judgment. The crucible moment hangs on their judgment, for better or for worse. Consequently, the risk is high.

Differentiation

Each of these case studies is also unique.

- Each is wholly unrelated to the other and implicates dramatically different situational contexts;
- They involve different sets of actors with different backgrounds, experiences, and training; and

- They occur at unrelated times spanning three decades.

It is from this perspective of differentiation that allows us to identify and test the deeper codes and common patterns that exhibit themselves in critical moments.

Observations

This experiment reveals several overarching observations:

There are strong correlations between these deeper codes and common patterns for leadership in crucible moments.

Understanding these codes and patterns can inform our own analyses and actions.

We can build upon these strategies, lessons, and techniques.

They should be integrated into our own exercise of judgment.

In doing so, we will lead from insight and strength.

Our judgment will become exceptional in our own crucible moments.

We will better ourselves. We will better others.

How to Read This Book

This book is structured in a way that will feel vaguely familiar to those who have had the dubious pleasure of attending law school, yet it is designed to be highly accessible to leaders of all backgrounds.

The first part sets forth three distinct fact patterns. These fact patterns provide characters and context. They establish what is happening above the waterline in the various crucible moments, but also tease at the tensions and drama at play subtly or not so subtly below. We become sensitized to the situational context facing leaders in their moment of challenge, as well as the dynamics of whatever game of strategy and chance is being played.

The second part digs into the characteristics, proclivities, and patterns of leadership in crucible moments, using the three fact patterns to illustrate the opportunities and pitfalls that emerge in crucible moments of decision-making.

The third part of this book is an overlay. There are ninety callouts that describe the deeper codes, common patterns, strategies, tools, and methods for your use in both preparing for and exercising judgment in your crucible moments. Each of these callouts is numbered and correlate to a comprehensive mind map that readers can download for use in developing their own playbooks.

THREE CRUCIBLE
MOMENTS

The Height of the Cold War

1986

Three hundred meters below sea level,
somewhere off the coast of Vladivostok, USSR

Sixty men lie still in the dark. They are dressed in their working blues. Their shoes are on. They try to sleep but cannot. They listen, hour upon hour. On a more ordinary day, they filter out the hum of motors, the sound of air pushing through vents, the chatter of the other men like them, the tinkle of silverware dancing on the metal trays in the mess, and the groan of the nuclear submarine as it snakes through the water.

Not now. Everything is perceived. Their own breath sounds of thunder as it passes in and out. They feel their blood swell and their throats grow tight. They listen for sounds that do not fit the patterns long established in their minds, such as the slightest deviation from the ordinary screams and murmurs of the machine. They operate on instinct, matching what they perceive to the patterns they know and discovering what they do not. It is in this latter gulf where their fears tease at their bodies and minds.

The silence beyond them is immense. Their imagination spins, searching for clues that might tell them what they most wish to know: *Are they hunting, or are they the hunted?*

In this moment, they are more than ordinary. Their powers are now immensely greater, heightened by the sharpened edge upon which they sit, making the delineation between their strength and their vulnerability indistinguishable. All these men know for certain is that a penance will be paid if they fail in this moment. The risk is that they will not return to shore as victors. The risk is that they, as men in a cold vessel, will die violently. Their vessel and their bodies will quietly sink to the bottom of these godforsaken waters in which the enemy prowls. The risk is that they will be the trigger point for a greater war the world fears, all because they may fail to perceive well, react well, or think well in this crucible moment.

Commander T. W. "Ted" Hack stands silently in the control room of the USS *Guardfish* (SSN-612). He, too, is watching, listening, and thinking. He and the crew are submerged somewhere in the dark waters just off the Petrovka Naval Base and Shipyard near Vladivostok, the headquarters for the Soviet Union's Pacific Fleet. In this moment, Hack, this machine, and its men are the tip of the spear of US naval strategy.

The battleship had defined naval warfare in World War I. The aircraft carrier did so in WWII. It is now the nuclear submarine that dictates advantage in the Cold War.[1] The decisions Hack will make in the coming hours will determine nothing less than the advantage gained or lost between nations. These decisions will be his alone, for there is no one to call or ask permission of when you command a submarine underwater. The commander makes the go/no-go decision when the moment demands it. One such moment will soon be upon him.

The Americans had long held an advantage over the Soviets in submarine warfare.[2] Yet in the early 1980s, this advantage was quickly slipping.[3] The submarine was the centerpiece of Soviet naval strategy. In fact, 60 percent of the Soviet naval

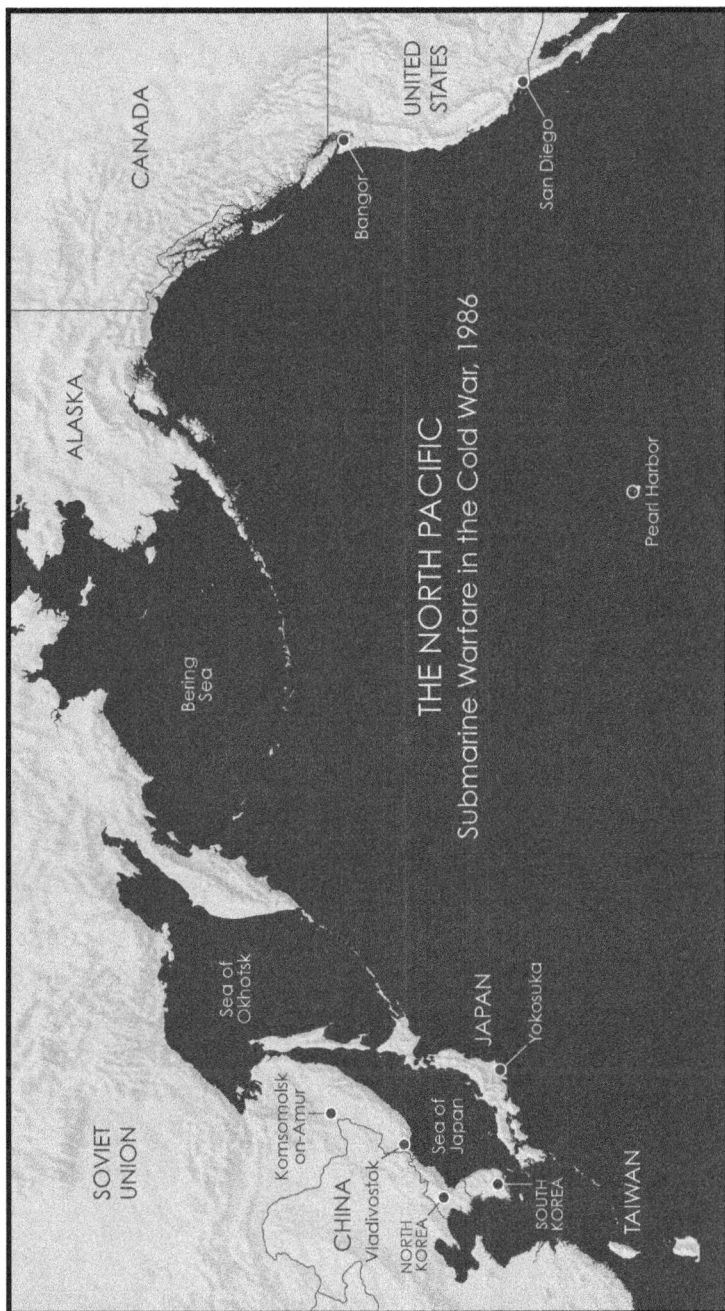

THE NORTH PACIFIC
Submarine Warfare in the Cold War, 1986

CANADA

UNITED STATES

Bangor

San Diego

ALASKA

Pearl Harbor

Bering Sea

Sea of Okhotsk

SOVIET UNION

Komsomolsk on-Amur

CHINA

Vladivostok

NORTH KOREA

Sea of Japan

JAPAN

Yokosuka

SOUTH KOREA

TAIWAN

budget was dedicated to submarine warfare.[4] Their submarines were also bigger, faster, and could go deeper than any American submarine.[5]

Their strategy was to now go even bigger and become even bolder. Soviet shipyard capacity, already more than double that of America's, further increased.[6] The pace of new subs coming off the Soviet lines stepped up markedly, particularly for nuclear submarines.[7] The Soviets sought to own dominion over the Barents and the Kara Seas to the northwest and the Sea of Okhotsk on their Pacific Coast.[8]

They built submarines that could patrol under the Arctic Ocean, hiding undetected in the vertical crevices created by the ice, able to break through and strike the United States at its north.[9] Soviet submarines crawled outside Charleston, South Carolina, and Bangor, Washington, to monitor new American submarines coming out of shipyards.[10] Soviet commanders became more aggressive, and, in some cases, either intentionally or inadvertently collided their vessels with American surface ships.[11] More precipitous to the rising tensions, Soviet submarines were outfitted with more nuclear arms, and those arms could now operate with substantially greater speed, range, and accuracy.[12] A long-range nuclear missile launched by a Soviet submarine from the Sea of Okhotsk, the patch of water nestled behind the Kamchatka Peninsula and just above Japan, once took twenty-eight minutes to travel four thousand miles before hitting a target in California. Now it would take only six.[13]

Something else was of greater concern to the Americans. In the early 1980s, naval intelligence witnessed a new generation of Soviet submarines launching from shipyards in the Baltic Sea and the Pacific Ocean.[14] Satellite imagery revealed the submarines emerging from construction bays at key Soviet shipyards. American submarines and other antisubmarine warfare capabilities were deployed to track the new

Soviet vessels as they submerged. The Soviets' Victor III, for example, slipped into the water after it was introduced, then simply disappeared.[15] Something had changed. The game was now different. The Americans sought to know why.

The Americans had believed they held a twenty-year technological lead on Soviet submarines.[16] The Victor III dispelled this notion overnight. The Soviets now appeared to be on par with American engineering.[17] They could credit these advancements to several spies; they had turned several Americans willing to betray their country. Beginning in 1968, a US Navy communications specialist began providing intelligence to the Soviets. In the 1970s, that specialist, John Walker, along with navy veteran Jerry Whitworth and several others, supplied the intelligence that convinced the Soviets they needed to aggressively advance their acoustic strategies.[18] The Walker/Whitworth spy ring revealed the Sound Surveillance System (SOSUS), the United States' secret weapon for superiority during the Cold War.[19] The SOSUS referred to arrays of hydrophones set along the seabed that could passively detect movement by Soviet submarines at long range. Coupled with intelligence from aircraft, surface ships, and submarines, the Americans could typically account for all Soviet submarines in the Atlantic Ocean and the Mediterranean Sea at any time, and those in the Pacific and Indian Oceans much of the time.[20]

The long-running American strategic advantage lay in its ability to hear Soviet submarines as far as a thousand miles away while remaining undetected.[21] Every submarine possesses an acoustic signature, which is a composite of sound waves it emits while operating. American sonar listened for certain narrowband, low-frequency tones transmitted by Soviet submarines while maneuvering.[22] These tones could be emitted, for example, from the way the propellers of the submarine cut through the water. The composition and patterns

of these emitted tones then enabled the Americans to identify what lay out in the darkness of the sea, whether it be a
migratory whale, a fishing trawler, or an enemy submarine.
Conversely, if strong, narrowband tones are not emitted, the
submarine moves undetected.[23] The Soviets were striving
quickly to attain such stealth.

On November 21, 1983, the Central Intelligence Agency
(CIA) issued a classified intelligence report on five nuclear-powered submarines in various stages of Soviet development, along with information pertaining to their propulsion
systems.[24] "The information was acquired from a Soviet with
a technical background and good access to the information,"
the report states, affirming that the Americans had their spies,
too, willing to betray the Soviet motherland. "A new submarine class called the Akula is also mentioned" by the Soviet
informant, according to the CIA report.[25] This becomes perhaps the first known report of the Akula within the US intelligence community. Some analysts comforted themselves by
believing it would take another decade for the Soviets to fully
engineer, construct, and launch Akula submarines.

Known as the Shchuka-B or Project 971 class, the Akula
was being built at the Severodvinsk shipyard on the Kola Peninsula in northwestern Russia and in Komsomol'sk-on-Amur
in the Russian Far East.[26] The Soviets were dramatically advancing their submarine engineering. They had historically
excelled at engineering for the speed, size, and depth of their
subs; now, they focused on acoustics, which had been their
weakness. Instead of mounting their turbines directly to the
hull, a traditional technique that transmitted significant vibrations in the water that could be heard by American sonar,
they adopted the technique of engine "rafting."[27] Here, powerful engine turbines would be suspended from the internal
hull and hung from isolation mounts. This greatly quieted

vibrations. It was a technique likely taken from the Americans' own engineering of their Thresher-class submarines, like the USS *Guardfish* itself, now hovering in waters off the Petrovka naval shipyard. The Soviets also acquired Western technology, most notably advanced milling technology from Toshiba of Japan and computer control systems for such equipment from Kongsburg Våpenfabrikk of Norway.[28] This technology helped the Soviets remedy their greatest weakness in the water, that being the noise their submarines' propulsion systems generated as they cut through the deep.

The Komsomol'sk shipyard lies some 350 nautical miles inland from the Sea of Okhotsk, the Soviets' protected bastion on its Pacific flank and the long-running playground for gamesmanship among the Cold War powers.[29] One of the more significant gambits in the ongoing game of cat and mouse was code-named Operation Ivy Bells by the Americans.[30] It had been critical to American advantage in the Pacific. The Soviets had eliminated the advantage just several years prior.[31]

In January 1980, American Ronald Pelton walked into the Soviet Embassy in Washington, DC, and offered to sell what he knew from his work with the secretive US National Security Agency (NSA). From 1980 to 1983, the Soviets paid him $35,000 for those secrets, including disclosure of Operation Ivy Bells.[32] The Soviets had run an undersea cable through the Sea of Okhotsk to connect their naval base at Petropavlovsk on the Kamchatka Peninsula to the mainland headquarters for their Pacific Fleet in Vladivostok, then claimed the Sea of Okhotsk as territorial waters. Foreign vessels were prohibited from entering. The waters were well patrolled by the Soviets and the location for many of their military exercises. As part of their defense, the Soviets installed listening devices along the seabed to detect intruders, including US submarines and surface ships.

At some point in the 1970s, the United States was able to attach an apparatus around the Soviets' communication cable four hundred feet below the surface of the Sea of Okhotsk.[33] This listening device allowed for eavesdropping on the communications among the major bases of the Soviet Pacific Fleet. The intelligence was invaluable. It let the Americans understand nothing less than the full extent of the capabilities, strategies, and movements of Soviet submarines, nuclear weapons, and intercontinental ballistic missiles. The advantage was lost when the Soviets removed the listening apparatus in 1981 based upon the information that the spy Pelton provided them. The Americans were left in the dark.

Piece by piece, the Soviets leveled the playing field below the waterline. As the power of the two foes equalized, either in reality or in perception, submarine warfare edged closer to a trigger point.

By the winter of 1985, the Soviets had edged ahead in terms of sheer brawn, speed, and strength. Their weapons could strike from longer distances. The advantage of the SOSUS passive, long-range sonar was significantly eliminated; wholesale eavesdropping on the Soviets' Pacific operations was gone. The Cold War was a long-enduring and high-stakes game of chess between the United States and the Soviet Union, each moving their pieces to provoke action and reaction, to increase the pressure, and to force errors, hopefully without triggering nuclear annihilation.[34]

They came close;[35] the game had become one of near equals. For the Americans, now deprived of their intelligence operations to maintain advantage from a long range, they now could go in only one direction to reclaim asymmetric advantage—*closer*.

The Americans would direct their submarine commanders to get close to the enemy—*physically*. US Navy Adm.

James D. Watkins revealed in 1984 that American submarines had been entering Soviet bastions,[36] saying, "[The Soviets] know we can get in their knickers before they can find us, and they don't like it."[37] The strategy was similar to a press defense in basketball, going man to man, increasing the intensity, harassing the enemy, and seeking to force errors. From a larger strategic perspective, it was a necessity, the way to track the increasingly stealthy Soviet submarines when long-range, passive sonar approaches were neutralized. It kept those subs closer to the motherland in a defensive posture rather than allowing them to move out offensively to taunt US Navy ships and ports or to lurk along American coasts and outside the mouth of such ports as Bangor or San Diego. It was also necessary to lay eyes on a machine that had become so quiet so quickly.

The strategy was dangerous. Any single aggression or mistake by a commander could spark global nuclear annihilation.

Komsomol'sk-on-Amur

The city of Komsomol'sk-on-Amur, where the new Soviet submarines were being built, owes its existence solely to the designs of Communist industrialization policies. In the early 1930s, Soviet planners determined to build a center for industrialization in the midst of the undeveloped timbers, ores, and fuels located in this remote eastern region of the Soviet empire.[38] In 1932, the Soviets founded the city, transferring thousands of members of the Union of Communist Youth—the Komsomol—to the area to construct a city at a bend in the Amur River.[39] The location was also chosen because it could be defended. Upstream, the northward-flowing river forms a significant portion of the Soviet-Chinese border. After passing Komsomol'sk, the river flows northward another 350 miles before dumping into the Sea of Okhotsk, which in turns feeds into the Pacific Ocean.

The city was built on the backs of forced labor, including waves of common criminals, political prisoners, Japanese prisoners of war during WWII, and Russian soldiers who had been POWs of the Germans in WWII and were sent to a Stalinist colony in the east upon their return home.[40] The city was closed to foreigners until 2003; it was not marked on Soviet maps.[41] It was, however, one of the Soviet Union's primary centers for shipbuilding and aircraft construction, including for military purposes.

During the winter of 1985, thousands of Komsomol'sk workers would have trudged day after day, night after night, through the frozen city streets to reach the shipyard and its six construction bays.[42] Underneath the steel roofs of those halls, shrouded in the secrecy necessitated by the Cold War and the paranoia woven into the culture of a city founded for this purpose, they would build the vanguard of Soviet submarines. American satellites would photograph the shipyard on regular passes overhead, hoping for a day free of gray clouds and a glimmer of what lay within. Steps away from the construction yard, the Amur River would be frozen over. Once the spring air started to push out the cold, the ice would begin to fracture.[43] The waters once again would become navigable; boats would dart about their tasks. Logs would float carefree, cut from the forests upstream and now flowing toward the mills below.

In April and early May of 1986, imagery analysts at the CIA would have noticed something else: Workers would start to dot the yards outside the construction halls; exterior docks would be set up with new configurations; different equipment would shuttle around. The activity signaled a new submarine would soon launch.

A temporary dock for the launch would be flooded to lift the submarine from its station. The undercarriage of equipment that cradled the submarine during its construction would be removed and the waters allowed to pour in, bringing them level with the Amur.[44] The submarine would then slide into the Amur like a crocodile's quiet entry from the bank into a river. Collars similar to buoys would be installed to surround the new vessel and protect it from the logs competing with it on the float downstream.[45]

In May 1986, only two and a half years after the first classified intelligence identified the new Akula as being in production, American imagery analysts[46] come to know three things:

A new Akula is in the water.

It is a beast.

It will soon hunt Americans.

The new Akula navigates under its own power from the shipyard along the muddy and winding Amur to its mouth 350 miles downstream.[47] The Soviet approach to launching new submarines from the Komsomol'sk shipyard would be similar to building American submarines in an inland town not listed on any maps sitting along the Arkansas-Louisiana border, then floating those vessels down the Mississippi River to the open waters of the Gulf of Mexico.

At the mouth of the Amur, the Akula turns south into the protective cove nestled between Russia and Sakhalin Island on the east. At the bottom tip of the island, the land's range dips underwater, reemerging less than thirty miles farther south as Japan on the Akula's portside. US Navy patrols by air and sea launched from bases in Japan are watching. The Akula stays close to the Russian coast as it moves south. It then

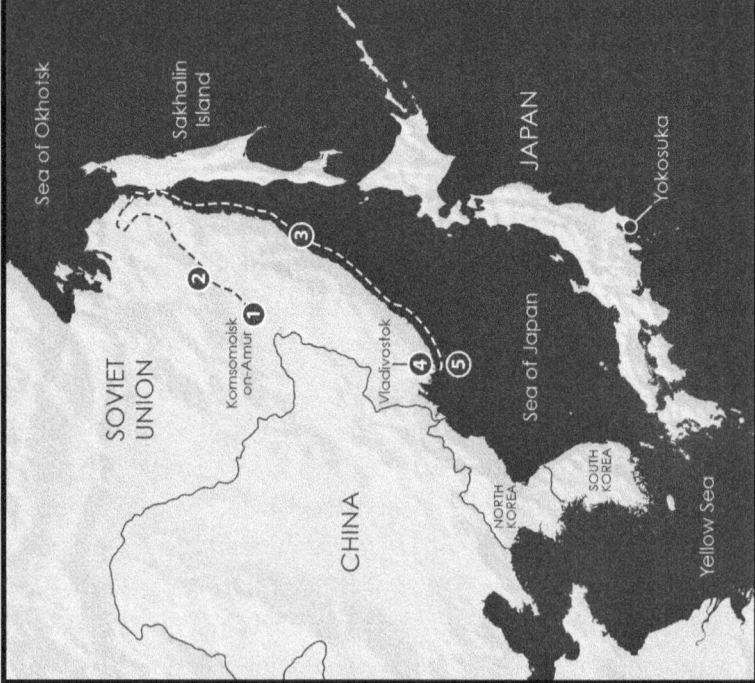

HUNTING THE AKULA
May–June, 1986

1. Akula being built in Komsomolsk-on-Amur. Satellite photography notices changes in dock configuration: Preparing for Akula movement: April–May 1986

2. Akula floats down Amur River (northward flow): 350 miles to opening into Sea of Japan near Sakhalin Island; satellite imagery May 1986

3. Akula hugs Soviet coastline in the Sea of Japan; American patrols from Japan tracking

4. Akula fitted out with final systems at Petrovka Naval Shipyard

5. Akula launched for its inaugural sea trials, May 28, 1986

Sea of Okhotsk

Sakhalin Island

JAPAN

Yokosuka

SOVIET UNION

Komsomolsk on-Amur

Vladivostok

Sea of Japan

CHINA

NORTH KOREA

SOUTH KOREA

Yellow Sea

turns westerly toward Vladivostok and docks at the Petrovka shipyard, whose primary purpose is fitting out, repairing, and overhauling nuclear submarines for the Soviets. After its final fitting-out, the Akula will navigate into the waters of the Sea of Japan for its trials.

The Americans will then begin their pursuit.

The USS *Guardfish*

Commander Hack took command of the USS *Guardfish* in August 1985.[48] For the past nine months, he and the crew would have been busy carrying out training and operations throughout the Pacific theater. Every so often, sometimes in the daylight but most often in the middle of the night, Hack would take the submarine to periscope depth. It is a routine maneuver but a dangerous one, as the underwater craft often cannot see what is above it as it rises. There are numerous instances where vessels collide before or after surfacing because of the lack of visibility. The maneuver is also risky in that it can expose the submarine electronically, as the burst of satellite transmissions potentially becomes a beacon that can reveal the location of the submarine to the enemy.

Sometime in May 1986, Hack would have ordered the USS *Guardfish* to periscope depth. He would then have received word that the Akula was on the move. It would be a surprise. The Soviets were bringing the Akula-I class of submarine to sea in one-third the amount of time US intelligence analysts had projected. It was to be the next great leap in Soviet submarine strategy.

The Soviets had seemingly achieved acoustic parity with their launch of the Victor III in 1978. By 1985, the Americans had improved their techniques and technologies in order to reliably track the Victor III. With the launch of the Akula, however, parity was once again lost. The threat was great. In fact, the Soviets may have finally achieved both engineering and acoustic superiority over the Americans. Furthermore, all of these gains were made at a time in the arc of the Cold War when the game was moving faster, the threats had become more significant, and the stakes were getting higher. In the game played between the superpowers over the last four decades, the next move on the chessboard would be that of a single man and his crew.

Hack received his orders. He then slipped the USS *Guardfish* below the waterline. It was now his turn. He would get closer. He would hunt the Akula deep in Soviet waters. He would have to get in her knickers.

On May 28, 1986, the Akula launches from Petrovka shipyard for its sea trials, the final step before its commission as a war-going vessel.[49] The USS *Guardfish* sits deep in the waters somewhere near the shipyard. Satellite imagery would have provided some fragmentary clues as to what the crew would face. They know the Akula is about 362 feet long. If set inside a National Football League stadium, it would reach from beyond one goalpost to just beyond the other. The breadth of its hull would cover the hash marks down the middle of the field. The USS *Guardfish*, by contrast, was substantially smaller.[50] Its matchup with the Akula, in terms of size and girth, would be the equivalent of asking a five-feet-two-inch American basketball player to post up on a six-feet-nine-inch Soviet version of LeBron James.

Lacking physical or technological superiority, Hack would have to rely upon the skills, perceptions, and reactions of the crew of the USS *Guardfish*. These men had devoted their careers to learning this complex, lethal machine. They had practiced the routines. They had mastered the techniques. They had memorized thousands of pages of engineering schemes, manuals, processes, and maintenance procedures, and they knew what to do in an emergency, in an attack, or in a retreat. They would have been tested over and over, sometimes on paper, sometimes orally, and sometimes in a spot check with a superior officer, designed to be random, surprising and conditioning the right responses under stress-inducing conditions. They were qualified against the high standards set by the nuclear navy and then tested some more.

Over roughly ten months on board, they would have worked into the rhythms of a team, whereby every man comes to know the other deeply. They would have drilled together, eaten meals together, and played cards together. They would have lived weeks and months together in quarters so intimate, they knew one another's scents. They could tell each other apart by the sound each made while asleep. They would know how to get a smile. They knew whom each man had left back home, whether a wife, a girlfriend, a daughter, or no one at all. They knew how each individual man thought, behaved, and would react under different conditions.

They communicate with one another in a language purpose-built for operating and living aboard a nuclear submarine. They will then communicate even more through a look, a motion, or the energy they carry. They will move together in silent orchestration, with efficiency and the knowledge of what they can expect from all others in this submerged vessel of humanity. They know whom they can trust with their thoughts. They know whom they can trust to perform when it gets tough. Their greatest weapon cannot be spied from a satellite overhead or an informant who walks into an embassy to sell secrets. Instead, this ninety-man crew now hovering in dark waters in the Sea of Japan together forms a weapon of advantage. They are the intangible. They will determine who will win and who will lose in the game that lies ahead.

Hack stands in the darkened control room. The entire boat is quiet. The calculus of the go/no-go decision rests with him. This will be his test. In the coming hours and days, he will be required to make a string of such decisions that will determine the fate of this vessel, the men on board, and perhaps the Cold War.

Some heroes achieve stature in our eyes from their public deeds. However, the men and women of the US Navy—and particularly, submariners in its nuclear navy—work quietly and without public commendation. Their missions are classified. They are the unsung who prepare to execute the decisions that define our history and our lives in ways we likely will never know. The public record of exploits by men like those of the USS *Guardfish* is minimal. Their actions have been state secrets, part of the asymmetric advantage military strategists seek to leverage and retain for their power and to preserve the greater peace. All we know for certain about the USS *Guardfish*'s exploits is from a public report stating simply, "*Guardfish* returned from a most successful six-month Western Pacific deployment in January 1987."[51]

The Akula's Secrets

But with the passage of time, the release of classified materials, and the piecing together of scraps of information from a myriad of sources, what can be surmised is that over the course of several days in late May or early June 1986, Commander Hack and the crew of the USS *Guardfish* likely surveilled all the secrets lying in the darkened Soviet waters. Hack likely ordered the submarine to come in close to the Akula while it was on its inaugural sea trials, tucking in below, bobbing along its sides, then dropping back and around the propulsion system. All the while, the crew pushed their "five-feet-two-inch" vessel to its physical maximum, losing parts of its surveillance capabilities due to the stress placed on the machine and the daring with which they pursued the Akula. The USS *Guardfish* indeed got into the Akula's knickers.

Over the course of several intense days, the Americans lurked in the shadows and then struck, navigating in close to discover the Akula's deepest secrets. The USS *Guardfish* took advantage of the vulnerabilities of a new boat and a new crew. The Americans photographed all of the Akula, including that which had been hidden below the waterline. They learned of the Soviet advances, including a new propulsion system with a seven-blade design milled with Japanese technology that allowed it to move through the water without emitting the sounds the Americans used to track enemy boats.[52] The Soviets had also modified the hull design to improve hydro-dynamic flow around the boat.[53] They had further muted the boat by adhering rubberized tiles to its exterior that reduced drag and noise.[54] The crew even discovered that the Akula's limber holes, where water is allowed to pass inside its outer hull when diving, were covered with retractable covers to minimize acoustic output.[55]

The USS *Guardfish*, by preparing for this moment, working into the intensity instead of shying from it, regained the American advantage in the great game. It did it on the first day or two of the Akula being out in the open waters near Vladivostok. The Soviet Union crumbled three years after the exploits of the USS *Guardfish*, broken by the larger game. Four decades of Cold War would end.

The Precipice of Global Economic Collapse

2008

"We conclude this financial crisis was avoidable. The crisis was the result of human action and inaction, not of Mother Nature or computer models gone haywire. The captains of finance and the public stewards of our financial system ignored warnings and failed to question, understand, and manage evolving risks within a system essential to the well-being of the American public. Theirs was a big miss, not a stumble. While the business cycle cannot be repealed, a crisis of this magnitude need not have occurred.

"To paraphrase Shakespeare, the fault lies not in the stars, but in us."

The Financial Crisis Inquiry Report:
Final Report of the National Commission on the Causes of the
Financial and Economic Crisis in the United States
January 2011

On September 12, 2008, the world's economy teeters on the precipice of collapse. It is late on a Friday afternoon. Several dozen men gather in Lower Manhattan. The economic equivalent to nuclear annihilation may be triggered in the next several hours or next several days. The decisions these men will make or fail to make in this time will affect the lives of billions around the world.

The men summoned to the Federal Reserve Bank of New York, or the Fed, are titans of finance.[56] They include the chief executive officers who run Goldman Sachs, Credit Suisse, Merrill Lynch, Morgan Stanley, and Citigroup, along with their chief financial officers.[57] The Fed building is fourteen stories tall and fills a city block in the heart of New York's Financial District. Below ground are another five stories, excavated down to the very bedrock anchoring the island of Manhattan. Within this subterranean chamber sits bar upon bar of gold, each weighing twenty-eight pounds. It is the world's largest repository, all kept safe for thirty-six other central banks around the world.

If the Fed is the castle of American finance, the men arriving are its chieftains, summoned from across the empires of American and, for that matter, global finance. Tonight, they will be called upon to lay down their arms in the grinding battle that plays out daily among them, at times essential to one another's success, while at other times engaging as fierce enemies. They will be called upon to subvert their ordinary selves in service to a higher, collective good.

Timothy Geithner, president of the Fed, and Henry "Hank" Paulson, the secretary of the US Department of the Treasury, meet with the chiefs to discuss the fate of Lehman Brothers, at once their brethren and a competitor. Lehman lies bloodied and wounded from the unfolding meltdown of the financial markets. The prognosis is dire. Lehman will not make it to Monday morning's opening bell.[58]

Geithner and Paulson implore the chiefs to find a way among themselves to rescue the situation so as to prevent the hemorrhaging financial system from going into full arrest.

The case is made that if Lehman fails, each of their institutions will suffer irreparably. The implosion of one could consume each in the aftermath.

Geithner and Paulson were taking a beating for rescuing Fannie Mae (the Federal National Mortgage Association) and Freddie Mac (the Federal Home Loan Mortgage Corporation) only five days earlier, pledging $200 billion to comfort the markets. They had taken political hits earlier in the year for orchestrating the rescue of Bear Stearns.[59] They reasoned that government intervention was not stanching the negative tide. In fact, the markets were growing ever more panicky.[60] Furthermore, putting taxpayer funds at risk to bail out the problems of rich men in black sedans was a hard sell. The political risk was too great. The regulators and the bank chiefs who had gathered all knew something else as well:

It was going to get worse before it got better.

There was really only one question to answer at this point:

Who would step into the breach:
the banks or the taxpayers?

Geithner and Paulson state in no uncertain terms that the government will not use taxpayer funds to save Lehman. The government will not provide any guarantees. It will make no capital injections. It will not harbor the riskiest assets.

Geithner breaks the chiefs into three working groups for the evening, schoolboys given their assignments, charging them to figure it out themselves.[61] They stay until 9:30 this Friday night. They come back with no resolution other than to return Saturday morning.

While the fate of Lehman hangs in the balance, a second

meeting is simultaneously underway in the castle. Senior executives from the global insurance corporation AIG are briefing other Fed officials on their current state. The meeting has been called hurriedly. A helicopter was supposed to have ferried the AIG executives into the city, but gusty winds and rain forced it to ground. Instead, a black sedan had to navigate slow southbound traffic from sleepy Wilton, Connecticut. As the car pulls into New York's Financial District, the AIG executives see office workers from the banks and exchanges bustling to catch their trains home. Gray light darkens the narrow streets in the shadows of the pillars of finance.

The AIG driver pulls up to the Italianate fortress of the Fed, squeezed between Liberty Street and Maiden Lane, joining a procession of other sedans delivering the chiefs for the first meeting, somber men in suits, each uncertain of the fate that would unfold inside.[62] The tragedy of the terrorist attacks of September 11, 2001, had occurred seven years and one day ago just four blocks to the east, forever changing the course of history. Tonight may as well.

AIG is the largest insurance company in the world. Its headquarters is a scant two hundred meters from the Fed. AIG's struggles over the past several years were well known in the capital markets and among the regulators. The Fed had been monitoring this crisis and had intensified its inquiry into AIG's health over the past several months. Because AIG is largely an insurance company and not a bank, however, there is little that the Fed can do or will do to help it right the ship. It will only watch.

AIG's treasurer tells the Fed that it has only five to ten days of liquidity remaining.[63] At the front line of AIG's liquidity battle is its subsidiary, AIG Financial Products, known in financial circles simply as FP. Jon Liebergall, who manages FP's liquidity, has accompanied the treasurer to the meeting. Over the past year, Liebergall has been at the front of a failing war to stanch FP's financial implosion. Before he speaks, the treasurer tells him, "Don't sugarcoat it."[64]

FP's business focuses largely on derivatives, including those on interest rates, currencies, equities, and commodities. At the most fundamental level, the company sells insurance on portions of the financial risk exposures held by others, although the derivatives could also be used for leverage, to manage regulatory capital exposures or, quite frankly, simply to skim a profit by arbitraging a pricing inefficiency in the market. Liebergall's job was to manage the cash coming in with the cash going out of FP across this diverse book of business. For the past year, it was going out faster than it had come in.

"Eight billion dollars," Liebergall tells the Fed officials, describing the FP capital hole as of this night.[65]

It is bad news. It is going to get worse. The commercial paper market is now closed, he says. AIG is no longer able to roll over its paper. The repo market is closed. Cash is depleting quickly. Asset prices are plummeting.

The credit rating agency Standard & Poor's has put AIG on watch status. Unless AIG shores up its capital positions over the weekend, it will get a ratings downgrade on Monday. Under the terms of AIG's derivatives contracts, a ratings downgrade will set off another slew of capital calls by counterparties. There had already been billions in calls over the past year, much of which were by the chiefs down the hall pondering Lehman. FP had been able to negotiate down the demands along the way, as well as find sources of cash to cover the onslaught. The pace and size of the calls, however, now arrive exponentially faster. In addition to the current hole Liebergall faces tonight, if S&P downgrades AIG on Monday, he estimates counterparties will issue another $8 billion to $10 billion in capital calls immediately.[66]

AIG's defense can no longer be held.

The Foreshadowing

Fourteen months earlier, Liebergall is in another meeting, just down the street, this time at AIG's world headquarters. The offices sit just a stone's throw from the Fed in a building known simply as 70 Pine.

Liebergall leans in close to Joseph Cassano's ear. Cassano is the CEO of FP, the elite financial unit otherwise tucked away in a nondescript, two-story brick office building in Wilton. "Goldman is making a collateral call," Liebergall says. Cassano does not understand.[67]

It is Thursday, July 26, 2007. Cassano thinks it must be a mistake. Every counterparty knows that AIG never puts up collateral.[68] It is one of the cardinal rules of the game.[69] AIG is a financial behemoth, a beast, a titan leveraging its power to harvest profit, a privilege bestowed upon the most powerful and the most cunning in the shark's game that is global finance. The lions of global finance, such as Goldman Sachs, eat first, demonstrating another of the game's unwritten but no less cardinal rules of the events now unfolding.

As a subsidiary, FP is the tip of the spear for AIG's financial innovations. Cassano is the steward of FP, an elegant money-printing machine that generated profits of 45 percent in 2004 and 83 percent in 2005. Best of all, Cassano and FP believe the machine prints money virtually risk-free, later stating it was "hard for us, without being flippant, to even see a scenario within any kind of realm or reason that would see us losing one dollar in any of those transactions."[70] FP had been mining various veins of gold for several years now, none more profitable than the contracts it had written in the US housing sector.

Cassano's main objective is to ensure no one interrupts the hum of his glorious machine, not even the prestigious heavyweight at the pinnacle of finance, Goldman Sachs, which has the apparent gall to demand FP immediately transfer $1.8 billion as assurance FP will make good on its contracts.[71] The demand surprises Cassano and his team.[72] It also surprises Liebergall, who stewards the daily flow of funds into and out of FP on its diverse book of business.[73] Finding $1.8 billion to appease Goldman Sachs's skittishness was not on his radar. It never needed to be.[74] It is one of the cardinal rules.

To understand Cassano and the decisions that lay before him in the moments and months ahead, it is necessary to understand the immensely complex game being played. There are rules, principles, and behaviors that guide a process in which literally trillions of dollars move across millions of transactions knitting together the complex ecosystem of US housing finance. These rules set the powers of the respective players, as well as their limits.

For example, yet another cardinal rule of the larger game is that an individual player can see only that which is around them, never the full realm of the game. There are domains and dynamics that are unknowable, unattainable, opaque, and even mysterious to each individual player from their unique vantage point.[75] There will always be things they cannot see but others can. Even the overseers of the game, a mishmash of federal

---

1 A player's blind spots can be exploited for advantage.

---

and state regulators, lack visibility into the full breadth of the realm.[76] They lack an understanding of the intricate and arcane behaviors of a game unfolding, pushing into new reaches at the edge and into the darkness. In some cases, regulators will pronounce they know how the game will unfold and how the players will behave. This is not true. Their prognostications will be proven wrong. They are just as blind as all the others.

Some of the known rules of the game are written, of course. There are laws, regulations, and the actual terms of contracts executed between counterparties. These rules consume millions of pages if compiled into a single compendium.

There are, however, vast quantities of unwritten rules. They might describe how the titans exercise systemic power in the financial system and orchestrate the labor of minions. They would explore the perceptions and biases of the individual players calling the shots at critical moments, twisting whatever events might otherwise come next to reflect their individual worldviews, beliefs, and values, inflecting the game for everyone else in sometimes mysterious ways. Still others would

---

2 Decision arcs flow in response to the rules of the game, which are both written and unwritten, overt and subtle, static and dynamic.

---

describe how markets rise and fall upon the ethereal emotions of traders, the media, and analysts, and with everyday people in places like Tulsa and Tacoma playing with their 401(k) accounts, reveling in the thrill that attracts the masses to bullish markets rising or causing them to scatter when the fear of contagion lurks in the shadows of the forest ahead. If descriptions of these powerful and dramatic forces that act upon the game were distilled into the codicils that truly determine its ebb and flow—and ultimately determine those made victorious and those vanquished—they would consume millions of pages more.

Because of these complexities—and despite what the

smart guys in the game might tell you, including the regulators, ratings agencies, and traders—it is not possible for there to be any true master of the game. The mysteries prove elusive to all, even the most powerful, the most cunning, or those who believe they are closest to the source of the secrets.

Those who succeed in the game are instead those who interpret its inflection points with greatest acumen. These

---

3 Those best able to understand the dynamics of how the rules behave, including when they set the game, change it, or are suspended, will possess a higher probability of success than their competitors.

---

inflection points occur when there is a sudden change that exposes something not previously known or that could not have previously been seen. It is within these inflection points when the rules morph, new behaviors emerge, and others fade away. They expose cracks of light that open opportunities for some while shunting others. Some of the players perceive these inflections. They sense the opportunities. They attune to the threats. Others do not.

Goldman Sachs's demand for $1.8 billion from FP is one such inflection point. Cassano must divine the new rules unfolding. Everything is now different.

Precursors

The origins of this particular inflection point in the financial markets are rooted in four precursors.

The first occurs in the 1990s with President Clinton's objective of promoting homeownership as a passageway to the

American dream. It was a noble and admirable goal, so much so that George W. Bush continues the policy when he assumes the presidency in 2001. The complex web of government regulators and government-sponsored enterprises each fell in line to do their part in serving the greater good. The Federal Reserve kept interest rates low to help expand the economy and make mortgages more affordable. The banking regulators loosened lending standards to enable more people to become homebuyers. Fannie Mae and Freddie Mac spun their machines to keep the housing finance markets well lubricated so that their staggering growth continued unimpeded.

Simultaneous with the transformation in the housing market, major change was underway in the financial services market, providing the second major precursor to this moment. US banking regulators were deregulating the financial services industry, arguing that free market forces would act as self-regulators, punishing those who acted excessively, compulsively, or inappropriately. Congress agreed, comforted by the assurances of the revered economic helmsman, Alan Greenspan, the federal reserve chair who had stewarded the American economy through its tough patches and exuberances for nearly two decades. The economic prophet promised that responsible institutions had the will and the way to police themselves.

As the regulations and oversight gave way, innovative new financial techniques were introduced into the market, allowing money to flow more freely, searching for emerging new places to harvest returns. The third precursor was in the trillions of dollars that amassed in the so-called shadow banking system, swirling in a parallel universe outside the realm of government oversight and regulation.[77] A significant portion of the swirl was in the trading of derivatives, those complex financial instruments that the major regulators and Congress had purposefully excluded from regulatory oversight just several years prior.

The fourth precursor was in the development of the technique known as securitization, which enabled financial engineers to slice and dice pools of assets like a butcher breaking down a carcass to separate the expensive cuts from the cheap, the filet mignon from the burger. Through securitization, engineers created a stratified series of investments from a common pool of assets, each sliver calibrated to meet the unique risk-to-return profiles of diverse sets of investors. Securitization enabled more and more investors to participate in rapidly growing and unregulated markets, finding whatever cut suited their individual appetite and their pocketbook.

A Tiny Slice

The relatively mundane world that had existed for decades in writing mortgages for homeowners was transformed by the convergence of these four precursors, each amplifying the tremendous growth of this market. By the early 2000s, a new, more robust supply chain for financing homeownership had emerged. The chain began with thousands of new mortgage brokers coming into the game, all searching for prospective homeowners in need of financing. Once identified, millions

---

4 New learning curves are created with each new development in the decision arc.

---

of homeowners were then shuttled through the mortgage underwriting process with a bank. The banks would then sell the mortgages to underwriters, which are the large investment banks on Wall Street. The underwriters would aggregate vast quantities of mortgages to create a large pool of assets structured into a single, investable bond. They then sold this bond to large institutional investors looking for a predictable payment stream.

Sometimes the bonds they created would blend the underlying mortgages with other types of assets, such as credit card receivables, student loans, auto loans, or even aircraft leases. These multisector bonds were designed to reduce the payment risk by diversifying the underlying pool of assets. If one sector became distressed and there was a rise in payment defaults, the other unaffected sectors would still perform, and the payment stream to investors would continue unimpeded.

Underwriters then began going a step further with securitization, engineering discrete allocations of these bonds into individual, marketable financial investments purpose-built for different types of investors, some wanting super-secure but low-return investments and others wanting higher-yield but riskier investments. Some buyers wanted filet mignon, while others wanted hamburger.

As the next step, these underwriters would take each slice to third-party ratings agencies such as S&P or Moody's, which would then evaluate the slice and certify its quality.

With these developments, the supply chain was transformed, unlocking its potential for growth, which it did exponentially. As it grew, however, it required a continuous source of raw material as input. The machine needed even more mortgages on the front end. It also needed more buyers of the slices on the back end. Between the front end and the back end of this new supply chain, a whole ecosystem of brokers, banks, ratings agencies, and service providers emerged to take a snip of the action, charging fees along the way, incentivized to do more of whatever they do: finding prospective borrowers, writing more mortgages, underwriting more bonds, slicing and dicing them into more pieces, or selling them to more buyers.[78] It was a virtuous circle of growth for every player. As long as the underlying assumptions this vast and beautiful machine was built upon held true, it worked. It also worked as long as the scale and

---

5 The individual's and enterprise's abilities to compress new learning curves as quickly and efficiently as possible creates advantages and reduces vulnerabilities to competitors.

---

reach of its supply chain continued to grow, expanding to new edges, including its riskier ones.

FP played a very specific role along this supply chain. In order to make one slice in the stack more marketable to buyers on the back end of the chain, underwriters such as Goldman Sachs, Credit Suisse, Merrill Lynch, J.P. Morgan, Bear Stearns, and others needed to make the collateral debt obligations, or CDOs, extremely secure from the risk of loss, including the risk of default on repayment of the underlying mortgages or loans. FP wrote a contract promising that it would cover the losses if there was a credit default on the underlying pool of assets. It provided this protection not as a regulated insurance company, which FP was not, but on the implied promise that comes from parent AIG having a massive balance sheet and an AAA rating from the ratings agencies.[79] The promise implied that AIG's heft meant it would likely be one of the last standing after everyone else had been decimated in a market crash.

The promise, however, was naked. FP held no reserves to cover potential losses. It was neither a bank nor an insurance company required to maintain reserves. Instead, if there were losses, it would have to make good on its promise by figuring it out later. It is the sort of promise that could be made only in the swirl of the unregulated, shadow financial system where FP operated rather than the regulated insurance business of its parent.

FP and AIG were comfortable making this promise because they believed it to be what they called *structurally hedged*. The truth is, they never thought they would suffer such a loss. They believed it was near impossible.[80]

This structural hedge was built upon several core elements. First, FP's credit default swap business was built upon mathematical models developed by a Wharton School banking and finance professor and FP consultant, Gary Gorton. These models used decades of historical data and predicted, with a 99.85 percent confidence level, that FP would take no losses on the credit risk it assumed, even under economic conditions as dire as those during the Great Depression.

Second, FP helped determine the pool of underlying assets in the bonds it backed. When the underwriter put together the transaction, they provided FP with a long list of the assets they proposed to aggregate into the pool. FP would send this list to a credit analyst in London and identify any specific assets they felt were too risky. These then were excluded from the proposed pool.

The process of sorting assets to improve the quality of an underlying portfolio worked somewhat like a High Plains cattle trader who buys one hundred twenty head of cattle from a dozen different ranchers. The cattle are a bit of a hodgepodge. Some weigh twelve hundred pounds, and some weigh eight hundred. Some are yearlings, and some are six years old. Some have been finished well on green grasses and golden grains. Their meat will be richly marbled. Others have had to forage on poor, rocky land where only the scrub grows. Their meat will be tough and rangy. It will not meet the expected standard of high quality.

After the cattle trader has assembled this pool of mixed and matched cattle, a buyer from the meatpacking plant comes out to take a look. He tells the cattle trader that twenty head of the cattle are of such poor quality he will not take them. These are sorted from the pool of one hundred twenty in order to keep the quality of the remaining pool high.

To continue the metaphor, the cattle in the pool are slaughtered, leaving one hundred carcasses hanging from hooks on a rail in the plant. Butchers get busy slicing the carcasses down into component parts. Each cut is sorted into separate piles, ranging from the premium cuts of steak down to the hamburger made of remnants. Of all the meat now amassed into discrete piles based upon its quality, FP only cares about one: filet mignon.

The third element of FP's structural hedge is that it writes its promise to provide credit default protection only on the prized cut, the filet. In financial terms, this cut is known as the *super-senior tranche*. The likelihood of default on this small cut from the larger pile of carcasses is extraordinarily low.[81]

Furthermore, this small slice of the pool is taken to S&P or Moody's to grade its quality independently. Let's say it receives an AAA rating. The process, again metaphorically, is similar to that of a USDA meat inspector now certifying the quality of a cut of meat, stamping it with a seal in purple ink to indicate it meets a qualified inspector's highest standards. FP writes protection only on these AAA-rated cuts.

FP then goes even further. The fifth mechanism to limit its risk is to establish a specific attachment point for the risk it assumes.[82] Typically, FP's obligation to pay on a loss would not arise until after a certain loss threshold has been met. This means there could in fact permissibly be some spoilage in the stack of filet mignon, but FP's obligation to cover losses would not arise until after 15 percent to 20 percent of the pool spoils.

FP's structural hedge encompasses this full array of mechanisms, which collectively reduces its projected risk of loss to virtually nil. With this method, the structural hedge is attained through a combination of actuarial analysis, portfolio selection, financial engineering, and legal drafting.

For this protection, FP is paid a small premium of around twelve basis points.[83] Twelve basis points is not much. If the notional value of the underlying pool of assets in the CDO was valued at $1 million, then the buyer of the protection would pay FP the modest sum of $1,200. However, FP could realize $300 million in high-margin revenue if it wrote $250 billion in protection with a risk to FP of virtually nothing. It did the latter.

At massive scale,[84] FP had built a beautiful machine.[85]

Something Shifts

In 2004 and 2005, Wall Street was hard at work, slicing and dicing tranches of multisector CDOs into myriad pieces, earning billions in fees doing so. Alan Frost of FP was the go-to guy on Wall Street for the major underwriters to get a credit default swap written on the super-senior tranche. In late 2005, Cassano promoted Frost to a new post, essentially a minister without portfolio, charged with leveraging the relationships he had built with Goldman Sachs, Merrill Lynch, J.P. Morgan, Credit Suisse, and others. Cassano gave Frost the mandate of finding new veins of gold for FP to mine with the big boys of Wall Street, just as he had done with the credit default swaps on the multisector CDOs.[86]

To replace Frost, Cassano asked Gene Park to take over the multisector CDO desk.[87] Park had sat in the same Wilton office as Frost. He also wrote credit default swaps, albeit exclusively on bonds by highly rated corporate issuers.[88] Park did not know much about the US housing sector or the multisector CDO book, despite it being the sister desk within FP just a few paces from his own. There was an air of secrecy about the two desks, even within FP's small office in Connecticut. He asked Cassano for some time to do his own diligence before taking the job.[89]

FP was a unique business. It took, for example, hundreds of thousands of employees to manage AIG's regulated subsidiaries. In contrast, it took only four hundred to manage the unregulated FP subsidiary. Furthermore, the team managing the multisector CDO desk was tiny.[90] Frost ran the desk and was the face to the underwriters.[91] Adam Budnick executed the transactions. A single credit analyst in London looked at the proposed portfolios as they came through. A single lawyer, Jake Sun, drafted the paperwork, a relatively routine task due to the base agreement using a standard document from the International Swaps and Derivatives Association. Cursory summaries of the deals passed to the parent risk-management group at AIG for review.[92]

For managerial oversight, Cassano stayed extremely close to the desk with daily and at times hourly calls to Frost. Yet a deal worth billions in notional value would be touched by only five or six individuals along the path to its execution. This group was tightly connected. Their communications were intentionally close and guarded,[93] doing customary internal reporting and nothing more.[94] Cassano was a micromanager. He was also a known tyrant, prone to aggressive outbursts and bullying behaviors.[95] Park, despite being an insider on the FP team, would have to be delicate in his attempt to get an eye into FP's multisector book.

Park began studying the recent trends in the US housing market and was shocked. It was no secret that there was a deterioration in standards at each step of the supply chain, as many analysts pointed to emerging problems. Park wanted to get deeper inside the multisector book to gauge FP's exposures. He pulled aside Frost's lieutenant, Budnick, in the Wilton office for a quiet conversation.

Park was concerned that the underwriters were slipping poor-quality meat into the underlying pools, contaminating the larger pool. Budnick stated that he believed the new pools of assets being brought to market might have a few low-quality assets tucked into them, but not more than 10 percent to 20 percent of the overall pool.

Park asked him to dig deeper. He suspected the lieutenant was executing the transactions but did not really know what were in the instruments. It would be hard to do such diligence meaningfully, given the small team size and the exponential growth in deal volume in recent years. In years past, for example, Budnick and the multisector CDO team might process a new deal every month. By mid-2005, the machine had grown to processing a dozen in a month.

Budnick pulled Park into a conference room days later and closed the door. He had done the research. He was shocked. The pools of assets were no longer abundant with filet mignon. Instead, 80 percent to 90 percent of the underlying pools consisted of ground hamburger from old cows. FP was writing protection on lower-quality assets with a higher risk of default. Yet it was getting paid only twelve basis points for taking this risk, just as it had when writing protection on high-quality credit risks.[96]

Park flew to London to tell Cassano he would not take the job. Cassano exploded. He thought Park was simply being lazy. Park returned to Wilton and did another several months of diligence. He later observed the risk he saw in the portfolio was too great, and he would not take the job. He stated, "I'm not going to opine on whether there is a train on its way. I just know that I'm not getting paid enough to stand on these tracks."[97]

He sent an email to Cassano in February 2006. It reflected the consensus of Cassano's team: FP should get out of the multisector CDO business. Cassano begrudgingly agreed. The decision to quietly withdraw from the CDO market should have made the path forward in the midst of deteriorating conditions in the housing market simpler.[98] It didn't.

The path had already grown treacherous, all while the multisector desk had been racing to close as many deals as possible without doing the diligence to really understand what risks lay within the underlying pools.

The machine was now spinning at such velocity, it would be difficult to stop.

Musical Chairs

At the beginning of his inquiry, Park felt in his gut the housing finance game was shifting. The reality is that it had already shifted.

Bonds backed by FP were based upon underlying pools having large portions of borrowers wholly unlikely to make payment on their mortgages. Vast numbers of these mortgages were structured on teaser rates, which involved extending to the borrower a low up-front interest rate they could afford, then converting it to a much higher rate two years after taking the mortgage. The expiration of the teaser rate and conversion to a high interest rate would naturally lead to a growth in defaults. The question was not if, but when. The cascade of defaults would ripple through the system. It was a ticking bomb.

For the titans of finance such as Citigroup, Goldman Sachs, Bear Stearns, Merrill Lynch, Credit Suisse, and AIG, similar realizations crept into their analyses. Players along the supply chain gradually came to the conclusion that the game had shifted from "got to get mine" to musical chairs, with no one wanting to be left holding risk when the defaults arrived.[99] Some naturally perceived the shift earlier and with more acumen than others. Some were slower or too vulnerable, too boxed in, or too intransigent to create an alternative path forward. For them, their likely fate was already cast.

The rules of the unfolding game of musical chairs are simple, clear, and draconian. When the music stops, one person will lose. The music will restart and stop again, over and over, with a player falling in each round until there is only one. To become the victor, the player must listen to the music carefully, gauging the right moment, positioning their body relative to the other players to get an angle on a chair for when the music stops. Some attune to this shift more quickly than others. Some see the angles for sliding their rear into a seat beneath the player in front of or behind them. Bigger kids and more agile kids have an advantage over those slower to perceive or less willing to push into the scrum. Like schoolchildren in the thrill of the game, the energy rises, and the line between excitement and fear is blurred. All friends now become foes. For some, the game will end in laughter. Others, in tears.

The big boys of finance defaulted to playing by the rules of a simple childhood game, some better than others. This would be no ordinary schoolyard version of musical chairs, however. The treachery of the game was immense. It would have several unique twists. First, it is an opaque market. The music is not playing in the gym for all to hear simultaneously. They have no common reference point. This is an unregulated market knit together by individual contracts and ratings agencies. Each player has to decipher the music themselves. They have to talk to their counterparts on the trades. They listen to whispers and rumors. They talk with the ratings agencies and see the deals

⬛6 Continuous intelligence-gathering is essential to understanding the unfolding decision arc

seeking passage flow across their desks. They talk with analysts, lawyers, and accountants who trade in part on being in the know. There is no public reporting. There is no oversight agency publishing what it sees from its perch, coaxing the parties to move faster or slow down. There is no exchange or clearinghouse that determines a common set of known rules among the parties. Instead, each player pieces together the music through their own unique filters. They hear notes, bars, and chords, but there are gaps in the sound and blind spots. Fears heighten as they question their perceptions and wonder if they missed the moment when the music really stopped.

The Bomb Maker's Vest

The second twist in this game is that the lights of the gymnasium are turned off for a moment while each player is fitted with a bulky vest. This vest has been created over the several years preceding this moment. It has many pockets, like that of a fly-fishing vest. Each pocket is filled with TATP, or triacetone triperoxide, an unstable, explosive cocktail used by terrorists.

The bomb makers are several. They are the brokers who found ordinary and unqualified people to take out mortgages. They are the mortgage finance companies that created all kinds of ridiculous mortgage structures that got people into mortgages that could be resold to underwriters. These included loans that required no evidence of jobs, income, or ability to repay (called *no doc mortgages* because they required no verifying documentation); adjustable-rate mortgages that started out affordable but later became expensive; or worse yet, mortgages based upon teaser rates that were both bait for unqualified borrowers and a lit fuse that would ignite the coming implosion. Underwriters such as Goldman Sachs, J.P. Morgan, and Merrill Lynch, who bought up these mortgages, pooled them together, sliced and diced them into component parts, and increasingly slipped poor-quality assets into new instruments.[100] Other bomb makers include the ratings agencies who stamped these pools with a seal, stating they were AAA-rated, regardless of the risks and remnants.[101] In effect, they collectively took dog food and sold some of it to the market as filet mignon.

All the pockets on all of the vests of all of the players were then interlaced with two wires, a black one and a red one. The black wire was the network of contracts that knit the financial players together. Thousands of contracts with hundreds of billions in notional value connected them as counterparties. The contracts allocated portions of the payment streams from the underlying bonds, as well as the associated risks. The argument was that the securitization and hedging techniques underpinning these contracts would enable capital to flow more freely, be put to better economic uses, and spread the risk across the broader system. The thinking was that if there were an isolated default, an individual party or two might be hurt, but the financial system could withstand the event. In other words, systemically, you could lose a firefight or even a small battle but still win the war.

The argument proved false. What happened, in fact, is that over the prior several years, the risks did not spread across the system as had been prophesized. Instead, the risks had concentrated among the largest financial institutions.[102] The black wires looped through them, connecting them together, intertwining their fate as the cascade of defaults loomed. As one institution failed, it risked triggering the next one's failure. There was another realization: FP had contracted with them all. If FP imploded, it could take everyone else with it.

The other wire—the red one—also laced through the vests but in a different way. The red wire was the leverage financial institutions had used to buy positions in the market. The major financial institutions borrowed money—lots of it—to play the game. In other words, some only had 50 cents in their pockets but could buy $40 of exposure through leverage.

Another simple cardinal rule is implicated by the use of leverage. When financial conditions worsen, leverage strains the borrower, sometimes a little, sometimes a lot. If the leverage is structured as a short-term obligation, a downward spiral can be triggered much more quickly than when the borrowings are structured as multiyear instruments.[103] Consequently, if the music stops abruptly, or even becomes just a bit scratchy, the market for short-term borrowing can quickly close out a player, starving them of the money they need to keep the continuous cycle of leverage running. The lenders fear the exposed borrower will default. The stressed institution may muddle through for a bit if they have cash coming in, either from other sources or from raising cash in the markets, that can settle those repayments coming due immediately. But their salvation might be for only several months, several weeks, or perhaps a few days, depending upon whether the markets stay steady, improve, or continue deteriorating. If the herd feels like the markets are weak or deteriorating, the strain leads to the agonizing process of culling the weak from the herd, and a willingness of the stronger ones to sacrifice others to save themselves.

In early 2007, the lights came back on. The music still played. The players, however, were lurching around the circle of chairs in their TATP-laden vests. It was a delicate dance.

The conditions were ripe for a triggering event. Mortgages were drying up. Underwriters were not putting new issuances out into the market. Every twig that snapped in the market risked spooking the crowd, sparking a meltdown. Countrywide went broke. Bear Stearns was sold under duress to J.P. Morgan Chase.[104]

Yet a few brighter moments in the music created a sense that perhaps the market would turn upward and regain its confidence, and the threat of negative consequences for bad behaviors would simply disappear. The bigger institutions, including AIG, were able to raise some $40 billion in capital to replenish their coffers. It gave them a bit more time to withstand a storm. It was a respite.[105]

It would be a short one.

The Mark

By July 2007, as the music played and Cassano and the financial titans danced around the circle, they sized one another up, looking for weaknesses, foibles, blind spots, tendencies, and tells. Part of the game was looking for their next mark, which is the weaker player to be forced from the game so that the others survive. In actuality, by this point in time, the mark may have already been made. It cannot be proven, and Goldman Sachs has always denied it,[106] but the circumstances would indicate that it "marked" Cassano and FP.[107] In the opaque market where the players moved in and out of the shadows, the collateral call shone light on a strategy of gamesmanship that had in fact been underway for nearly a year.

Goldman Sachs's game plan seems to have been put in place as early as 2006,[108] when as the first step, it packaged its remaining inventory of poor-quality deals, selling them to others in a market less attuned to the risks that lie ahead. It was moving risks off its balance sheet and onto that of others, buyer beware.[109]

Second, it began buying hedges for what risks remained, including protection against the risk that FP itself might default on its obligations.[110]

Cassano also had the opportunity to hedge FP's risk in 2006.[111] However, unlike Goldman Sachs, he and Frost elected not to do so.[112]

The rationale was simple: Buying protection mitigates financial risk. Buying protection is also expensive. Doing so would hurt FP's earnings. FP needed earnings. AIG needed earnings.[113]

Earnings were the lifeblood of Cassano's empire. They were his purpose and his identity. More specifically, by this point in time, AIG had renegotiated its deal with FP, harvesting 70 percent of FP's profits while FP retained the balance. Of FP's remaining allocation, which represented hundreds of millions of dollars in profits each year, approximately half was doled out among FP's four hundred employees in the form of extremely generous annual bonuses. Cassano personally determined these individual allocations.[114] It was his singular tool for engendering continued loyalty from a team he otherwise badgered to perform.

Cassano was also a career striver, the Brooklyn kid with working-class roots who had made it into the upper echelon of finance. He had given everything in his life to AIG and its emperor, CEO Maurice "Hank" Greenberg.[115] In doing so, he hoped for access to the most inner sanctums of privilege, access, and wealth within the AIG empire. Strong earnings kept Cassano in the arena, fighting for the chance of ascension.[116] If Cassano's earnings suffered, the upward trajectory of his career would end. The final chapter of his narrative would write itself. For Cassano to have a shot at one day being king, he would need to keep his run of exceptional financial performance going as long as possible.

The third dimension of Goldman Sachs's strategy was the collateral call, which was premised upon several developments that reveal the larger situational context, the behaviors of the players, and the outcomes that would unfold in the forthcoming year. The first roots back to the unceremonious dethroning of Greenberg as the chairman and chieftain of AIG in 2004.[117]

AIG had participated in several questionable financial transactions that misstated the company's financial performance. However, the incident was only partly about the financials. It was more significantly about character. Not only were the financial transactions themselves designed to overstate earnings, but during the investigation of these events, documents were destroyed by AIG personnel.

The investigation was led by New York Attorney General Eliot Spitzer, a climber in his own right. He elected to prosecute Greenberg, a heavyweight who had rarely lost a fight. Spitzer would not fight him in the courts, however. Instead, he would prosecute Greenberg's character through a trial by media. Winning in this forum is less about arcane laws and complex fact patterns. The methods are more about creating story lines, images, allegations, and inferences that the public can consume in thirty-second bites on television or in sensational, ten-word headlines. While Greenberg and AIG were warriors in the insider's power game of finance and litigation, they were much weaker when attacked in the court of public opinion. Greenberg, the "son of a bitch,"[118] as many knew him because of his win-at-all-cost methods, was immediately put on the defensive.

Greenberg's position was further hindered by a shifting framework for US corporate governance. Corporate boards were being empowered with independent supervisory powers in response to several instances of gross corporate malfeasance, most notably the failure of Enron Corporation, an energy, commodities, and services company. Congress had gone to work in the early 2000s to remedy the problems, enacting the Sarbanes-Oxley Act of 2002 to protect investors. As a result, corporate boards were required to empower independent board members with greater supervisory responsibility over the management.[119] Greenberg's historic board structure, more consistent with being a tribal council of elders who sat on the side and gave advice, was forced to give way to new members empowered to oversee the acts of management.

This new AIG board, facing its own headline-grabbing prospect of corporate malfeasance laid at Greenberg's feet, was forced to act. They ordered him to resign. He had erred in judgment, which as he knew all too well in the risk business was his fatal error.[120] Greenberg's legend, immense in the global financial arena, ended.

AIG also was forced to restate its financials as a result of this affair. When it did, the ratings agencies downgraded AIG from AAA to AA.[121] One of the implications of the downgrade, some three years later, was that Goldman Sachs was able to use the ratings downgrade as justification for the collateral call. A little-noticed and never-utilized provision tucked within the legal boilerplate of its credit default swaps gave them the right.

The Goldman Sachs collateral call revealed something else that had shifted in the game while the lights were low. FP's actuarial models looked at the likelihood it would suffer an economic loss due to defaults by the issuers of the underlying bonds. In 2007, however, a new accounting standard was being implemented known as *mark-to-market*.[122]

The new rule forced institutions to value assets on their balance sheets at their current value rather than actual gains or losses from trading in the market. In other words, companies no longer were on the hook to report economic losses they had actually suffered, but instead theoretical gains or losses based upon current market conditions.

The timing of the change could not have been worse.

In 2007, market conditions were eroding rapidly. Asset values would presumably erode as well, even in the absence of actual transactions. Institutions would be forced to report losses, even though there were no transactions. In fact, there was no viable way to actually value trillions of dollars in assets for which there was no public market, clearinghouse, public reporting, or volume of actual transactions in the market to provide a benchmark. The counterparties could go out to the market and do a dealer poll, essentially asking market makers for their best guesses on value. Without a viable trading market or public reporting on the asset class writ large, however, the poll would typically yield prices all over the board. It was guess-work—meaningless to making a fair determination of value.[123]

The last best alternative was for each institution to provide its own estimates as to the value of the underlying assets. What this did, in reality, was enable these individual parties to weaponize the valuation process.[124] In other words, they could use this policy change to tilt the rules in their favor in the absence of viable, market-based methods or other oversight. They could push into the gray area and search for a way to create asymmetric power over others.

Most notably, Goldman Sachs set its marks grossly lower than any other player in the market.[125] Over the past year, they had been making moves to short the US housing market. Now they were arguably using the mark-to-market policy as a lever to move the market further toward their bet.[126] They were controlling the music for the others in the game. They held the power.

Cassano did not see it coming. To counteract the power of Goldman Sachs's weaponization of the mark-to-market standard,[127] he did what he had always done—*negotiate*.[128] Cassano fought aggressively for months on end, arguing that the Goldman Sachs marks were much too low and therefore could not be used to force reported losses on the FP balance sheet.[129] He won small battles along the way, getting Goldman Sachs to reduce the amount of its collateral calls, gaining admissions from Goldman Sachs executives that they were "not covering themselves in glory," and finding evidence in their public remarks of the brazen game they were playing.[130]

Cassano, however, lost the war. The tit-for-tat battles waged on until November 2007, when the mark-to-market rule formally went into effect. At that point, there was no more

---

7 Winning small battles along a short arc may result in a loss in the long war being fought.

---

time on the clock to negotiate. AIG was forced to report unrealized losses on its balance sheet. The reported losses marked the beginning of the end of Cassano's long and successful career with AIG. He was asked to retire several months later.[131]

The mark was complete.

Return to 2008: The Sinkhole

Even though Cassano had been eliminated from the game in early 2008, the game wore on. Conditions continued to deteriorate. Fears rose. It had been fourteen months since Goldman Sachs had made its initial capital call to FP. It was a long slog in a war. The pace then accelerated. The long-feared end now began to feel imminent, increasing in intensity hour after hour, minute after minute.

A hotel room in Manhattan

Saturday, September 13, 2008, 4:16 a.m.

Jon Liebergall no longer knew how to sleep.

For over a year, since the first capital call, he could only close his eyes and drift off. Sometime soon thereafter, he would startle awake. Over and over, the cycle would repeat. This night had been no different. Perhaps even worse. It was now 4:16 a.m.

He always woke at 4:16 a.m. to check on the London markets. Movements in the currency, interest rate, and short-term liquidity markets over there sent the signal for the day he would face when the sun started to rise over here. Today was Saturday, though, and there were no markets to check.

His mind woke him, anyway. There would be no reprieve. Today would be another in a long stretch of marches toward the war's final front, each day full of skirmishes and firefights, wounds and losses, doors closing and options evaporating. He was certain today would be worse than the day before.

AIG had trillions on its balance sheet. But as of last night, it had only $9 billion in cash left. The corpus of the AIG empire was, quite frankly, healthy.[132] Yet because of the way the markets were wired together, with red wires and black ones intertwined in a dangerous if not reckless fashion, it might not survive next week. In fact, it might not survive Monday.

Liebergall let his mind drift off a bit longer before the sun rose over Manhattan.

70 Pine Street, New York City

Saturday, September 13, 2008, 8:30 a.m.

Liebergall steps out of the elevator of the Art Deco skyscraper onto a floor of conference rooms at AIG's headquarters. A few men mill about in golf shirts and sports jackets, a bit out of place on a Saturday morning on Wall Street. There is an uncertain energy among them. They survey who is here and who is not. By the end of the day, dozens upon dozens of executives will shuttle into and among the conference rooms. There are separate conference rooms to respectively deliberate each possible fate facing AIG: salvation financing, fire sale, or bankruptcy.[133]

The men hail from four private equity firms, four global corporations, three investment banks, two sovereign wealth funds, and the white-shoe law firms that seemingly represent any and all of the players, both individually and simultaneously. To a man, each is angling for opportunity, vultures smelling the hint of death along the highway.

---

8 **Identify the various trophies being hunted to reveal players' motivations, tactics, and likely next moves.**

The traditional rules on conflicts of interest are waived. Laws and norms for what comes next are thrown out.[134] Today will be about instinct, moving through the game quickly, deftly, and with cunning to survive the calamity all around, with the possibility of picking up some spoils of war only to emerge stronger on the other side. It is the fate upon which empires have long been built and long been lost. The men, their adjutants, and consiglieres whisper to one another in hushed tones.[135] The silent game of musical chairs, however, is blaring.

AIG is wearing its bomb maker's vest. It has $1.4 billion of its own commercial paper that needs immediate funding. Another $3.2 billion will come due next week. Lenders in the repo market are skittish. They currently hold $9.7 billion in overnight funding for AIG. As of last night, capital calls on AIG soared to $23.4 billion. AIG has paid nearly $19 billion on those calls, with $7.6 billion going to Goldman Sachs alone. Billions more could be demanded imminently, depending upon how the game unfolds over the next forty-eight hours. The ratings agencies, which will meet Monday, warn of imminent downgrades. Downgrades will trigger another $10 billion in collateral calls. AIG is also $24 billion short on the value between cash and collateral associated with securities lending by its insurance subsidiaries, another victim of the subprime housing market virus.[136]

Sunday morning, September 14, 2008

Saturday's AIG sessions were unsuccessful. The banks could come up with only $30 billion in financing, but the estimates for what AIG needs to survive the storm kept rising hour after hour, with one estimate reaching as high as $124 billion.[137]

Robert Willumstad, the new CEO of AIG who has been on the job for less than ninety days, tells Timothy Geithner that every meaningful pathway eventually requires government support in order to do more. Geithner says no.[138] Both sides seem to be playing chicken, with the viable players holding out until the Fed's position weakens and it agrees to take on the risk of loss.

In Washington, DC, Henry Paulson, who had spent the previous two decades at Goldman Sachs and was at its helm when it, too, became a major player in the US housing finance market meltdown,[139] meets with the White House. The crisis is dire. The potential for a messy failure is very high. Yet the Fed does not want to use its emergency lending powers set forth in Section 13(3) of the Federal Reserve Act.[140] The political ramifications of doing so would be awful.

If the Fed does invoke its emergency powers in this situation, it would effectively relieve those that have also engaged in risky behaviors. The argument is that saving Wall Street from its cycle of greed and irresponsibility amplifies the risk of moral hazard—that is, one's decisions and actions are disassociated from direct responsibility for the resultant and adverse outcomes.[141] The prophylactic to the problem of moral hazard is to punish the several so that in the future, others make less risky decisions.

As an alternative path, the banking regulators continue to argue that the 1998 experience of Long-Term Capital Management (LTCM), a highly leveraged trading operation, provides strong precedent. With LTCM, a consortium of banks acting without government financing or guarantees provided capital to LTCM to prevent the sinkhole beneath it from worsening.[142] The regulators argue that collaboration and self-sacrifice worked.

The chieftains are unmoved. They will not work collaboratively to save one of their own.[143] Not this time. Instead, they will cull Lehman Brothers from the herd. The cries of those wounded and dying due to the fate of Lehman will fade as the survivors march forward in their own quests for survival, or perhaps even gain.

For Lehman, the immediate focus is finding a buyer. Bank of America backed out of the Lehman acquisition conversations on Friday night. Barclays is now alone as the most likely candidate. Paulson lobbies Barclays, whose portfolio would be strengthened by owning a US investment bank. Barclays declines to provide salvation through an acquisition. More specifically, Barclays's UK regulator, the Financial Services Authority, blocks the purchase. The UK regulator states that it will not risk importing the "American disease" to the British Isles.[144]

Sunday, September 14, 2008, 3:00 p.m.

Christopher Flowers, a veteran of twenty years at Goldman Sachs who now has his own private equity firm, meets with Willumstad at his AIG offices.

Flowers describes himself as a "lowlife grave dancer."[145] This is the moment for which he waits.

He has arranged for a buyout of AIG's assets by Allianz, the global insurance conglomerate headquartered in Germany. AIG's share price closed on Friday afternoon at $12 per share. Flowers and Allianz offer $2 per share to acquire AIG. It is a sharp haircut. Allianz would then inject $5 billion in new capital into AIG. Allianz demands that it be shielded from AIG's liabilities. In other words, the offer to buy AIG requires the Fed to cover its liabilities.

Willumstad is unimpressed. It feels like theft. He asks Flowers to leave AIG's offices immediately.[146]

Sunday, September 14, 2008, late afternoon

The US Treasury tells Lehman it is letting them go. There will be no acquisition. There will be no bailout.

Lehman is instructed to file for bankruptcy. Lehman employees are seen leaving its offices with roller bags full of their personal possessions. They know the doors will be locked upon a bankruptcy filing and they will never return. Lawyers who have been idling pending an acquisition set to work, drafting the filing that will initiate the company's end.[147]

As Lehman is cut loose, any prospect of AIG finding a buyer also dies. No one will help.

Everyone focuses solely on their own survival.

Monday, September 15, 2008, 1:00 a.m.

Over the past forty-eight hours, Bank of America has been working through the calamity to add to its empire. Documents finally arrive from the lawyers to enable its acquisition of Merrill Lynch.

It is a coup of sorts. The genteel Southern bankers have at last acquired a prestigious Wall Street bank.

Flowers, the grave dancer, is paid $20 million to deliver a fairness opinion on the deal.

Monday, September 15, 2008, 1:45 a.m.

Lehman's bankruptcy filing is delivered to the court. It triggers bankruptcy proceedings in eighteen countries and the administration of some sixty-six thousand claims exceeding $873 billion in value.

As Lehman is sacrificed, AIG no longer controls its own fate. The whims of the game will determine its future.

Monday, September 15, 2008, 10:00 a.m.

Paulson returns to Washington, DC, from New York. He meets with President George W. Bush at the White House.

He then meets reporters in the White House Press Briefing Room. Policymakers and the media praise Paulson and the regulators for letting Lehman fail.

Monday, September 15, 2008, 10:30 a.m.

Lehman's bankruptcy sends the market into a spiral. The Dow Jones Industrial Average suffers its largest losses since the attacks of 9/11. Seven hundred billion dollars in shareholder value is immediately lost. The money markets experience a run in a phenomenon called *breaking the buck*.[148] Corporations cannot access the commercial paper market for short-term funding.

The sinkhole below the markets is growing larger.

Monday, September 15, 2008, 11:00 a.m.

Traders watch AIG as its share price plummets another 61 percent. Morgan Stanley loses 14 percent; Goldman Sachs, 12 percent.

Geithner calls the investment bankers to the Fed once again, this time to focus on AIG. Geithner asks J.P. Morgan and Goldman Sachs to put together a syndicate of banks to lend AIG $75 billion. He says once again that there will be no government support.

The banks set to work. They seek to raise $5 billion from each of fifteen banks to amass the $75 billion. In exchange, they will come to own 79.9 percent of AIG's equity.

AIG's shareholders will be obliterated.

Monday, September 15, 2008, 3:00 p.m.

S&P downgrades AIG by three notches. Moody's, Fitch, and other ratings services knock it down by two.

The downgrades trigger another $13 billion in collateral calls. Goldman Sachs alone immediately demands another $2.1 billion.

Monday, September 15, 2008, 5:00 p.m.

AIG makes $5.2 billion in payments on securities lending contracts. It informs the Fed that it can no longer access the short-term commercial paper market.

Monday, September 15, 2008, 7:00 p.m.

Goldman Sachs, J.P. Morgan, Morgan Stanley, AIG, the US Treasury, and the New York State Insurance Department reconvene at the Fed.

Talks surrounding a $75 billion syndicated loan collapse. AIG's problems are too big for the banks to solve. There will be no communal solution. Each player is on their own.

The opportunistic now pick at the carcasses of the others less fortunate for scraps of flesh.

Monday, September 15, 2008, midnight

Geithner wants to cut AIG loose. He is resigned to letting it fail.

He polls Federal Reserve staff members working in New York and Washington, DC, for their thoughts. They tell him that AIG is too big to fail. If AIG fails, it will pull down the others. They fear that when AIG's vest explodes, it will send a pulse that will trigger the explosive vests of all the others. The global financial system will collapse.

Tuesday, September 16, 2008, 2:00 a.m.

Geithner tells the Fed staff to go home.

Tuesday, September 16, 2008, 9:00 a.m.

Willumstad calls Geithner. He informs him that he is going to draw down all remaining credit lines available to AIG. It will be interpreted by the markets as a sign of desperation. The traders will push it down further. Bankruptcy is inevitable. "Don't do that," Geithner says. "I'll get back to you."[149]

Geithner wrestles with the momentous decision before him.

Tuesday, September 16, 2008, 10:00 a.m.

Willumstad has not heard back from Geithner. His back is against the wall. No relief is in sight. He gives the order to exhaust all remaining credit lines.

Tuesday, September 16, 2008, 11:30 a.m.

Geithner calls Willumstad to inform him that an emergency meeting is underway at the Fed. Willumstad rescinds the order to exhaust AIG's remaining credit lines. At the meeting, Federal Reserve chair Ben Bernanke and Paulson propose bailing out AIG.

Tuesday, September 16, 2008, noon

The Fed tries to prop up credit markets by injecting $70 billion into them. It has little effect.

The European markets begin spiraling, and its central bankers make calls to the Federal Reserve and US Treasury, asking that AIG not be allowed to fail.

Simultaneously, Paulson and Bernanke meet with Bush in the Roosevelt Room of the White House. Bush is in the final months before he leaves office, fatigued by nearly eight years of continuous war overseas. He tells Paulson and Bernanke to do what they need to do. He will support them.

Tuesday, September 16, 2008, a little before 3:30 p.m.

The sinkhole beneath AIG is spiraling out of control.

Geithner is losing the game of chicken he has been playing with the banks.[150] They will not concede to save one of their own for the greater good. The Fed will have little choice but to bail out AIG under its emergency powers.[151]

The decision will unleash a political backlash. Voters from ordinary places across America hate taxpayer money being used to fix the ills caused by the greed and abuse of the elite. Bailouts fuel the long-simmering cultural war within the American consciousness, stoking the tensions between the haves and the have-nots, the smart guys and the working class, those at the top of the pyramid and those who span across its base. Americans hated the bailout of Chrysler in the 1990s and the savings and loans in the 1980s. They will hate the bailout of the financial sector now.

The public will instead want, as it has wanted throughout the millennia, for there to be a hanging of those who caused this plight. Geithner, Paulson, and Bernanke will offer them AIG.

It is part of the ritual.

Tuesday, September 16, 2008, 4:00 p.m.

Security personnel from the Fed walk across the street to AIG's headquarters at 70 Pine Street. They collect the certificates to securities owned by AIG worth billions in the parent's stake in its subsidiaries.[152] They walk the certificates down the sidewalk back to the Fed. In a world where billions are at stake in abstract, unregulated, financial instruments that electronically traverse the global economy, the security the government desires is a bunch of paper certificates they will hold as collateral for a coming government bailout.

Tuesday, September 16, 2008, 4:30 p.m.

In Washington, DC, Bernanke and Paulson brief House and Senate leaders gathered in Senate Majority Leader Harry Reid's conference room. The leaders are informed that a government bailout is underway. AIG will be taken over tonight.

Tuesday, September 16, 2008, approximately 6:00 p.m.

The Fed sends the terms of the bailout to AIG. They use the term sheet developed by the chieftains when they were trying to raise a $75 billion syndicated loan funded by fifteen of their peers. The Fed has tacked on an additional $10 billion, just in case.[153]

Willumstad and his senior executive team are in his conference room. The terms are punitive.

The government will take 79.9 percent of AIG's equity, wiping out AIG's shareholders. The $85 billion loan will bear an interest rate of 14 percent, despite the market rate being only 1.5 percent. The loan will be secured by the assets of AIG. It will be required to pay the loan in its entirety within two years.[154]

Finally, Willumstad will be forced to resign. Although he has been at the helm for only ninety days, the crucifixion needs a face. It will be his. He will soon be replaced by Edward Liddy, a member of the board at Goldman Sachs.

The Fed states the terms are nonnegotiable. The funds can be arranged for transfer the next day to avoid further AIG defaults. AIG is given until 8:00 p.m. to make a decision.[155]

Twelve of the thirteen major banks still stand. They continue wearing their own bomb maker's vests. They now wait. They wait to see if the AIG crucifixion is sufficient to break the looming chain of explosions.

Tuesday, September 16, 2008, 8:00 p.m.

The AIG board votes. Ten of eleven members vote to accept the government bailout. AIG surrenders.

Tuesday, September 16, 2008, 9:00 p.m.

Three days after the Financial Services Authority blocked Barclays from buying Lehman Brothers, Barclays makes the purchase. By delaying until more of the music had played, Barclays not only avoids being infected by the "American disease," it is now able to feast upon the carcass of the failed Lehman.

Barclays buys Lehman at a wild discount, paying only $250 million for its investment banking assets and $1.5 billion for its Manhattan real estate. In three months, Barclays will revalue these assets at twice what it pays now.[156]

---

9 Some trophies are visible. Others are hidden.

Simultaneously, AIG pays out 100 cents on the dollar to every one of its largest counterparties.[157] It is another term of the sacrifice. In effect, the US government is bailing out all others in the game. Despite their having also worn bombmaker's vests knit together by red-and-black wires, they will not be sacrificed.

AIG transfers $63 billion to the other players in the game. Societe Generale receives $16.5 billion. Goldman Sachs receives $14 billion. Deutsche Bank receives $8.5 billion. Merrill Lynch, which has just been acquired by Bank of America due to its own dire consequences in running unhedged positions in the subprime market, receives $6.2 billion. Another twelve banks receive between $1 billion and $4.3 billion in funds to make them whole.[158] Everyone in the game left standing at this moment in time lives. Their vests are removed.

Their sins are absolved.[159]

Wednesday, September 17, 2008

The stock of AIG drops to $1.99 per share, a penny lower than where Flowers pegged it on Sunday when he was pitched out of Willumstad's offices. AIG has cumulative profits over the prior eight years of $66 billion. It will take $99 billion in losses in 2008 alone.[160]

Asian and European markets drop sharply. Trading in Russia is halted. There are runs on the money market funds. GE is closed out of the commercial paper market. Paulson talks with his successor at Goldman Sachs, Lloyd Blankfein, more than twenty times and with John Mack of Morgan Stanley twelve times over the next several days.[161] The closed-door talks presumably focus at least in part on defending against the short sellers targeting Morgan Stanley and Goldman Sachs in hopes of gains in the aftermath.

The sinkhole continues to widen.

The game shifts again. Geithner, Bernanke, and Paulson do in fact orchestrate the AIG bailout. They use their emergency powers. However, they need Congress to make the bailout stick. It is a tricky gambit.

If they ask for congressional help and the politicians reject the request—a very real possibility, given the electorate's fervid opposition to taxpayer-financed bailouts—the markets will react adversely. The sinkhole will only grow more quickly. There is little choice, though. The worst economic cataclysm since the Great Depression stands before them.

Congress enacts the Troubled Asset Relief Program (TARP). The markets rebound. The ad hoc, crisis-driven, ever-evolving game plan of Geithner, Bernanke, and Paulson is working.

2008 to 2010

What ensues over the course of the next two years is the worst financial crisis in global history, including the Great Depression, according to Bernanke,[162] the successor to the renowned Alan Greenspan who had been instrumental in creating the systemic conditions that led to this catastrophe.

Seventeen trillion dollars in household wealth evaporates within 21 months. Unemployment reaches 10.1 percent at its peak in October 2009, the worst since the Great Depression. Consumer and business spending ratchets down. Billions in additional government funds must be used to stem the tide and turn the economy around.

Bank of America, which acquired Merrill Lynch in the most critical hours of the unfolding crisis in a coup, takes another $90 billion in TARP funding. Citigroup, now relieved of its bomb maker's vest, takes $420 billion. General Motors and Chrysler, along with another one hundred fifty major corporations, file for bankruptcy.

The path taken was chosen by a handful of individuals closest to the crucible moment. They came as close to the edge as possible before working their way back out. They worked from instinct, leverage, and intellect to fashion the strategy.

They worked solely from their judgment in the moment.

The Global War on Terror

2015

Maren Brooks did not consider herself superstitious. She practiced being measured, disciplined, logical, fair, and wholly focused upon the mission before her at any given moment in time. It is her job.

It is 3:15 on a Friday afternoon. Today, the routine is easy. With a bit of luck, she will start the process of reading-in the next shift of officers who will monitor the world overnight. Once they take over, she will then navigate the afternoon rush hour out of Washington, DC; cross over the Potomac River via the 14th Street Bridge; and head into the normalcy of lives lived in the northern Virginia suburbs. She will put on some comfortable clothes, walk her dog, meet a friend for dinner, and have a glass of wine. It will be an ordinary evening, like the ones other ordinary people have. It is, however, Friday the thirteenth.

Brooks is senior director of the most sensitive location in the US government. The White House Situation Room does not look like much. It is actually a cluster of conference rooms nestled across the hall and behind a locked door from the White House cafeteria.[163] The ceilings are low. The seating is cramped. The decor is simple. On this day, it is quiet. That morning, her team had arranged a call between President Barack Obama and President François Hollande of France to discuss the upcoming climate summit in Paris in several weeks. This afternoon, she worked on updating the policies and procedures of the White House Situation Room, the living playbook by which this nerve center for US national security operates. It is continuously refreshed to reflect the learnings from experiences in which decisions are made in those crucible moments that do nothing less than define history.

PARIS

November 13, 2015, 9:16 p.m. Central European Time (CET);
3:16 p.m. Eastern Time (ET)

Six hours ahead of Brooks, Paris has come alive on its own Friday evening. Couples tuck into corner cafés for a night together. Revelers spill onto the sidewalks just beyond. Eighty thousand fans cram into the Stade de France in the Saint-Denis region north of the city, cheering on their beloved national soccer team challenging Germany, the current world champions.

Hollande sits in the stadium with his son,[164] enjoying a moment together wrapped within the spirit of sport, gathered among a French people united. As a symbol of *fraternité*, the German ambassador to France sits in the box near Hollande, friends watching their boys combat on a manicured pitch rather than the farm fields just beyond, as they have time and again in wars of the years before.

The joie de vivre of the French people connects as one spirit on this evening. Young boys catch the sight of their football-playing heroes. Lovers share bread and wine over candlelight in a corner bistro, and an elderly couple walks arm in arm along the sidewalk, relishing the waning days of a life lived well together. The November night air is crisp. The sky above the City of Lights is clear.

About seventeen minutes into the match, neither the French nor the Germans have scored. A few straggling spectators still enter the stadium. A young man in his twenties approaches Gate D on the east side of the stadium. He holds out his ticket to the game. A security guard pats down his jacket, just as he has done for the thousands of fans who passed through earlier.

The fans and workers still outside the stadium can hear the cheers of the crowd from within. This match is a friendly, meaning it will not affect the international standings of either team. Yet the French play with a grudge. Germany knocked France out of the prior year's World Cup. From there, the Germans went on to humiliate Brazil, the host country for the World Cup, with a 7-1 victory in the semifinals. They would then prevail over Argentina in the finals, bringing the crown home to Germany.

France has invested heavily in soccer for four decades. It has built its own beautiful machine. France supplies dozens of international-caliber players to the European professional leagues and more than a half dozen national teams. Those teams now compete at the highest levels of international competition. The French, however, sought change. They no longer wanted to merely manufacture players. They wanted to keep them home. They wanted to win.[165]

The roots of the French soccer development machine can be traced back to the decimation its cities and towns suffered at the hands of the Germans in WWII. Following the war, the country was largely in ruins. France had a labor shortage over the next several decades and recruited millions of immigrants to help with the reconstruction. The immigrant populations, drawn from the former French colonies of Morocco, Algeria, Tunisia, the Ivory Coast, Cameroon, and Senegal, settled into public housing on the outskirts of the heavily bombed cities.

At the same time these immigrants were helping rebuild France, they were building their own families. Their young children began to play soccer, and the best talent started to rise through the nation's soccer development system. It was a path for France's newest families to break out of the banlieues, those suburban ghettos where crime, violence, and rioting were high. Through soccer, young men could find a path to wealth and fame without regard to where they came from, their religion, or the color of their skin. The system is meritocratic. It works brilliantly.

As a result, fervently held notions of what it means to be French—as a people and a nation—begin to evolve. The French teams come to be known as the *black, blanc, and beur*— the Black, white, and Arab. French soccer development is now not only producing extraordinary players, but is provoking a societal shift in identity.

The fan at Gate D with a ticket in his hand and arms outstretched is of Arab descent, as is the security guard who pats him down. The guard feels something odd underneath the fan's jacket. The fan looks into the guard's eyes. The guard takes a step back. The fan then vaporizes himself in an explosion of blood, bones, hair, nails, and ball bearings.[166]

Inside the stadium, the crowd hears the explosion, but the match continues. The crowd assumes the noise is just fireworks from young soccer fans on a Friday night in festive Paris.

An aide whispers into Hollande's ear. The president stands. He tells his son to stay and watch the game. The president is escorted briskly out of the crowd.[167]

WASHINGTON, DC

Friday, November 13, 2015, 3:23 p.m. ET (9:23 p.m. CET)

The White House Situation Room is the central node within the nervous system connecting the diverse network of entities that collectively comprises the US national security apparatus to the president of the United States. It runs 24-7.

It is staffed by a small team of professionals drawn from the intelligence, military, and foreign policy communities. These personnel continuously monitor classified and unclassified information from around the world, looking for hot spots in the never-ending stream of global events. When one begins to flare, they start piecing together the best working assessment of the facts in an ever-changing, fluid environment. When a flare gets hot enough, they notify the president. Their job is to exclusively prepare for the momentous decisions often required of the leader of the country.

Within this network of governmental and military entities charged with protecting US national security, each department or agency possesses a unique mandate. Their power, however, is exponentially greater when they play well with one another. At their best, these sixteen entities knit themselves into one fabric that impenetrably protects the United States from security threats abroad and from within. In reality, it is an impossible mission. There is often conflict within this group. They compete. Their quest for power in service to their own mandates and aspirations often overcomes their capacity to act as one. When this happens, the common good suffers.

The worst threats—the most cataclysmic ones that reshape history—often emerge from the darkest corners. They emerge from new places, harboring grudges and worldviews that shape how someone can see a world so differently from ours. They search for our weaknesses, knowing that there is no way to win in a toe-to-toe battle with a powerful nation or its military. Instead, they look for those patterns and routines that make us susceptible to hidden vulnerabilities that may, under carefully selected and constructed situations, give them the momentary power to wound the lion where it is weakest. For example, the hard drives of terrorist leader Osama bin Laden that were examined after his assassination contained thousands of files and images he had gathered for his study of how the United States worked, including in the years following the 9/11 attacks. He was studying his opponent's playbook. He wanted to understand how we thought and behaved. He was looking for points of vulnerability and weakness he could further exploit, just as he had with the attacks that caught the United States wholly off guard. He was crafting his next playbook and looking for his next mark.

Opponents can heighten the vulnerabilities of those they seek to challenge. They do so by seeking to confuse the opponent's machinery charged with monitoring and responding to threats. They seek to surprise it. They spawn incomplete fact patterns. They use irrationality as an asset. They zig when the machinery thinks it should zag.

The vulnerability of the target is then amplified by the internal challenges created. The target weakens itself. There

---

10 Internal dysfunction when designing or managing the enterprise archetype increases its vulnerability and ability to effectively manage the decision arc before it.

---

will inevitably be poor internal communication, poor coordination, or inappropriate personal motivations, which come at a cost to the common good.[168] A spiral beneath begins to spin. The higher collective objective of protecting the nation's security is impeded. Judgment is clouded. Strategies are ill-conceived. Resources are misappropriated.

It is Brooks's mission to prevent any and all of these things from happening. She will do it quietly, diplomatically, without ego or emotion, from the small set of conference rooms in the

White House where President Harry S. Truman once had his bowling alley.

On this quiet Friday afternoon, Brooks is working on yet another of the continuous iterations to the playbook. It encompasses the policies and procedures for how the White House Situation Room works in conjunction with this network of sixteen national security agencies to respond to

---

11 **The player holding advantage is the one with the best playbook for decision-making under a myriad of situational contexts. This playbook intentionally optimizes the capacity for the decision maker to exercise exceptional judgment within each of these contrasting circumstances.**

---

threats. It is a playbook much like that used by an American football team. It embraces a game plan that can respond to a myriad of differing situations. It sets forth roles and responsibilities of the players and how they are to come together to interact and support one another so that the team's performance is paramount. It rests within three-ring binders, ready for the next flare-up. It reflects the team's best thinking on how to muster its power to win the game. It is continuously updated based upon after-action reports that are prepared on the heels of all major events, reflecting what worked well, as well as where the team broke down or was inefficient.

After-action reports for the White House Situation Room, a procedural step adopted from military combat teams, are designed to be brutally self-critical. When the team performs suboptimally, the problem most often ties back to how the team communicates, how it governs itself, or how it navigates from the murky gray of discovering what is true to the bright line required of presidential decision-making. In other words, how the facts are gathered and how the decisions are made most often determines whether the power of the US national security apparatus is at its greatest strength or worst vulnerability.

In thirty-seven minutes, Brooks will start the read-in of the overnight crew. In sixty minutes, she will drive out the southwest gate of the White House grounds. She might meet her friends at the cluster of restaurants off Beauregard Street run by émigrés who escaped Ethiopia's wars, famines, and genocide, or travel to Eden Center to share plates prepared by the elderly South Vietnamese restauranteur who fled when America's war in Vietnam failed a generation before. Brooks and her friends will talk about something other than the work they are prohibited from talking about, find a way to laugh, then return home to sleep.

In the middle of the night, she will check her secure BlackBerry when the dreams wake her to see if a hot spot has yet become an inferno or if she will be lucky enough to make a yoga session when the morning sun rises. She will try to drift back to sleep, the way ordinary people do.

PARIS

Friday, November 13, 2015, 9:25 p.m. CET (3:25 p.m. ET)

Hôpital Saint-Louis lies in the tenth arrondissement of Paris. It was established in the 1600s upon mandate from Henry IV. The grounds are pristine, with serene lawns and ancient trees arrayed along geometric walks, much like a walled park in the midst of the hustle and bustle of the surrounding Parisian neighborhood. Above the brick archway of the guardhouse to this oasis is etched the motto of the French nation: *Liberté. Égalité. Fraternité.*

A group of colleagues from Hôpital Saint-Louis gathers at a small café on Rue Alibert in the neighborhood just a few steps outside its southern gate. After a week of being extraordinary—doctors and nurses who tend to the needs of those hurting, ill, and dying—their Friday evening together allows them to momentarily revel in the simple joy of being ordinary. They feel the bond that reminds them they are human, whether from a shared laugh with friends, a flirtatious glance with another, or the feeling of life that can emanate from the elixirs served from the bar.

The neighborhood outside is alive. The crowds from Le Carillon, where the doctors and nurses gather, spill outside. They mingle with those from Le Petit Cambodge, a local Cambodian restaurant just across the street. The night air is punctuated by the sound of cheers and suffering as the crowds catch a glimpse on television of the French team's fate against the Germans.

A car pulls up outside Le Carillon. Two young men jump out. They point automatic weapons at the friends, lovers, and neighbors. They fire in bursts.[169] Bodies fall limp to the ground. Others scramble.

The men turn and fire on those gathered at Le Petit Cambodge.[170] The screams and confusion in the darkness continue. The men flee in a black sedan with Belgian tags.

The doctors and nurses of Hôpital Saint-Louis are no longer ordinary. They scramble among the fray, triaging the casualties, determining the dead, trying to stem the fate of the dying. In all, fifteen will die.[171] Ten will be critically wounded.

Now, somewhere outside the Stade de France, Hollande imagines the closed confines of the stadium, the potential to be a massive kill zone, and the fate of eighty thousand souls, including his son, at the mercy of the anonymous terrorists who have descended upon the city.[172]

The light from the stadium rises into the sky. The crowd's cheers can still be heard. Hollande must begin making his first set of decisions.[173]

Patterns

A mere eleven months before this evening, on January 7, 2015, gunmen stormed the offices of the Parisian satirical magazine known as *Charlie Hebdo*. Two brothers opened fire with assault weapons, killing eleven staff members, including the editor. They killed a police officer as they sought to escape the scene. Five hundred police officers were immediately activated to undertake a massive manhunt across Paris. The men evaded capture for nearly two days until police cornered them in a print factory near Paris-Charles de Gaulle Airport. An eight-hour standoff ensued, during which one of the brothers indicated they had been sent by Al-Qaeda in the Arabian Peninsula.

During the standoff, another man working in concert with the brothers walked into Hyper Cacher, a kosher grocery store, bearing a rifle, two pistols, and a submachine gun. He shot four people. He identified himself as affiliated with the Islamic State. He took fifteen hostages, telling police they would be killed if the brothers in the standoff were killed.

Around 5:00 p.m., Paris police launched flash bombs into the factory. The brothers emerged firing and soon thereafter died in a hail of bullets. Two police officers were injured. Minutes after the brothers were killed, police stormed the grocery and killed the armed man. All fifteen hostages were freed, but seventeen people died and twenty-two were injured.

Subsequent investigations of the men revealed the extent to which these incidents were part of a coordinated attack designed to maximize their impact. A video from the man who had taken hostages at the grocery emerged titled "Soldier of the Caliphate." These seemingly irrational attacks were the product of preparation, timing, and coordination. Their objective was to start with an attack, set a trap, increase the pressure, and increase the bloody losses. It was an intentional statement to the world. The nightmare threat of terrorists now racking up additional carnage raced through the minds of first responders and French leaders.

The earlier attacks in January also were part of a larger game plan unfolding from the murky shadows of a terrorist underworld.[174] Western governments studied each carefully. The *Charlie Hebdo*-Hyper Cacher attacks were followed in February by the stabbing of three soldiers outside a Jewish community center in Nice. In June, there was an attempt to blow up a factory in Saint-Quentin-Fallavier. In August, an ISIS militant smuggled an AK-47 and semiautomatic pistol onto a Thalys train bound for Paris with hundreds of rounds of ammunition. Several US military personnel traveling to the city apprehended him when his rifle jammed. There were other attacks occurring around the world claimed by organizations affiliated with ISIS. Two weeks prior to tonight, the Russian airliner known as Metrojet was downed, killing 224 people. Yesterday, suicide bombings in Beirut, Lebanon, killed forty-three people.

Several patterns emerged from this string of prior attacks. The terrorists sought to maximize the carnage in terms of lives lost. They were detailed planners. Sometimes the attacks were seemingly by an individual or a lone wolf. Increasingly, however, they were orchestrated by small teams of two to three individuals. These teams would act in concert with one another. Coordinating multiple teams required increasingly sophisticated prior planning, surveillance, materials acquisition, and handling, plus real-time communication during execution of the attacks. Al-Qaeda had stunned Americans with the sophistication of the surprise attacks on 9/11. The coordinated attacks by Islamic extremists from Pakistan on Mumbai, India, on November 26, 2009, revealed a sophisticated and purposeful level of psychological training, coupled with military and combat training. The pattern of attacks in France and elsewhere in 2015 demonstrated an increasing level of international coordination and communication by ISIS, which had once been discounted as being a lesser terrorist organization, a ragtag band of disaffected Muslims who lacked the ability to execute sophisticated attacks and, certainly, to expand outside of the Middle East.[175]

The motivations for each attack in 2015, however, had slightly different markings. The *Charlie Hebdo* attack was seen as retribution for its satirical treatment of Islam and Muḥammad. The Hyper Cacher was a kosher grocery.[176] The attacks in Nice were at a Jewish-owned factory. The Thalys rail attack was by an individual who apparently was motivated to kill Americans for retribution for the ongoing US military actions in Syria. The Metrojet bombing also was tied to Russia's involvement in Syria. The Beirut attack was by Syrians against Shia Muslim targets in Lebanon. For each attack, there were commonalities in the terrorists' motivations. There was not, however, a greater pattern. Each was too different from the other to provide any reliable indication to what would happen next or where. The strength of the terrorist game plan was its seeming irrationality. This preserved the element of surprise to their advantage.

Hollande and the French knew this. They began moving their pieces on the chessboard as if moving against an unknown enemy. The French moved with purpose and discipline. They sought to draw out clues of a trap being set. They hoped to not fall into one. They sought to preserve the lives of eighty thousand people inside the stadium and even more across Paris and France.

Hollande made his first series of decisions: Do not tell the crowd of the suicide bomber outside Gate D. Lock down the stadium. Tell the coaches and referees to continue play uninterrupted. Do not flood the stadium with police or first responders, who could fall into the trap of an unfolding kill zone. Send in a small, discreet team to investigate the scene. Listen and wait for what comes next.

Hollande did not yet know that an attack had been carried out just seven kilometers due south at Le Carillon and Le Petit Cambodge. Paris lacked a communication system to coordinate information and action across entities. In many ways, Hollande was flying blind. He was working on instinct. He would have to exercise his best judgment.

Another man walks toward Gate H of the Stade de France. He is playing his part in the game plan down to the designated minute. He detonates his vest of TATP. Like the one before him, his explosion can be heard by the crowds inside the stadium.

It is now clear that a coordinated attack is underway. One bomber worked to provoke fear and uncertainty in the crowd, forcing them to scramble and scatter. A second bomber intended to lay waste to them in the chaos of their flight from the stadium.

This second bomber, however, died alone. The crowds had been locked inside to protect them from the threat just beyond the gates. The terrorists' strategy was foiled. They were precluded from harvesting their additional dead.

Meanwhile, the soccer game carried on. The score was still 0–0.

WASHINGTON, DC

Friday, November 13, 2015, 3:31 p.m. ET (9:31 p.m. CET)

The analyst continuously scans the three monitors before him.[177] He is scrolling through internal messages, news feeds, and social media. He occasionally looks up at the news broadcasts on the televisions mounted to the wall in front of their workstations.

There are explosions in Paris. He begins piecing the fragments together. An explosion targets crowds at a soccer match between France and Germany.

Another slug pops up. There are shootings at two Paris cafés.

Another slug. There is a second explosion at the Stade de France.

This is no longer a quiet Friday afternoon. There will be no chance for Brooks or anyone else on the front lines of US national security to slide into an ordinary Friday evening. Instead, they begin the search for facts, patterns, and motivations. What trophies do these terrorists hunt? What will be their next move?

The normal protocol when a hot spot emerges somewhere in the world is for the White House Situation Room to start working through call trees to the various departments and agencies in the government best able to gain some insight into the situation on the ground. If the hot spot is within the context of an ongoing war or conflict, calls will be made to the US Department of Defense to get better visibility. If the incident is in one of the world's capital cities, a call is made to the US Department of State, which in turn activates the embassy and consulates to serve as observation posts.

These attacks feel different. They are escalating fast. They seem well coordinated. They are targeting masses of people, not a few individuals. These are not lone-wolf attacks. The expert predictions are wrong.[178]

The end point of this violence is nowhere in sight.

In this instance, the protocols inside the White House Situation Room begin to shift. Brooks instructs her team to open a conference bridge with the sixteen departments and agencies of the US national security apparatus: "Keep the lines open."

The events in Paris have the markings of a fast-moving, quickly evolving situation. Additional targets elsewhere in France, the Middle East, or the United States are a possibility. This might be a focused attack. This might be a decoy. This might be a ragtag band of radicals. Or this could be a sophisticated ratcheting up of the stakes by terrorist cells working together. This is all that can be surmised at this point. Anything further is presumptive, reflects a bias or agenda, or is a sheer guess.

The full power of US intelligence, military, diplomatic, and police power is spinning.

PARIS

Friday, November 13, 2015, 9:32 p.m. CET (3:32 p.m. ET)

The black SEAT Leon navigates the streets of the eleventh arrondissement. The Kalashnikov rifle lies beside the man's leg. He thinks briefly of those who martyred themselves eleven months before in this neighborhood, killing those at *Charlie Hebdo* who were infidels mocking the prophet. He and his brothers are prepared to martyr themselves tonight as well, certain to revel in the glory that surely awaits their own immortality.

The car comes to the corner of Rue de la Fontaine-au-Roi and Rue du Faubourg du Temple. He emerges from the car.

Soft yellow light emerges from La Casa Nostra and À la Bonne Bière. Families, friends, and lovers talk and laugh.

He shoots in short bursts. This is how he was trained. It is efficient. He sends bursts into the clumps of those now huddled in fear. Shadows fall limp. Five die. Eight are wounded.[179]

The sound of sirens screams toward the restaurants and the adjacent laundromat. The narrow streets become jammed tight. The gunman scurries into the darkness of the night.

WASHINGTON, DC

Friday, November 13, 2015, 3:34 p.m. ET (9:34 p.m. CET)

The public rarely sees those moments that lead to momentous decisions by leaders. Decisions made in crucible moments are the kind that tend to be made in closed conference rooms or quieter, more personal moments. When it is possible to get close to these moments, standing on the outside looking in, it is captivating.

We study for clues that help us understand what is at stake and how the decisions affect the individual. We look for expressions that reveal a tell. We study the way in which a person holds their body, gauging whether they feel they are winning or losing, attacking or being attacked.

One such moment occurred more than four years before this night on May 2, 2011. Obama had given the go-ahead for Operation Neptune Spear. US Navy Special Forces were authorized to enter Pakistan under cover of darkness and kill bin Laden. A photograph taken shortly after this decision captivated millions around the world.

SOURCE: Pete Souza, "Obama and Biden Await Updates on bin Laden," Creative Commons, http://www.flickr.com/photos/white-house/5680724572/, (May 1, 2011).

From left to right (seated): Vice President Joe Biden; President Barack Obama; Brig. Gen. Marshall B. "Brad" Webb (assistant commanding general of the Joint Special Operations Command); Deputy National Security Advisor Denis McDonough; Secretary of State Hillary Clinton; and Secretary of Defense Robert Gates.

From left to right (standing): Adm. Mike Mullen, USN (Chairman of the Joint Chiefs of Staff), Tom Donilon, National Security Advisor; Bill Daley, Chief of Staff; Tony Blinken, National Security Advisor to the Vice President; Audrey Tomason, Director for Counterterrorism; John Brennan; Assistant to the President for Homeland Security and Counterterrorism; James Clapper, Director of National Intelligence.

We see the inside of one small enclave in the White House Situation Room as some of the most powerful leaders in the world stare at a monitor. We search for clues as to whether they are winning or they are losing.[180]

Thirty-one years earlier, President Jimmy Carter gave the go-ahead for Operation Eagle Claw, an attempt to rescue fifty-two Americans held hostage in Iran. The operation was a gross failure, resulting in eight US service members dying and the hostages remaining hidden away inside Iran for another 271 days. Carter subsequently lost his bid for a second term.

Presidential elections often turn on something stirring in the psyche of the electorate. The fortunes of candidates rise and fall not so much with slogans, but with their ability to resonate with the electorate to salve the deeper psychological needs of the moment.

The deeper wound Americans were feeling during the 1980 presidential election turned on a perceived loss of their place of power in the world. Carter's opponent, Ronald Rea-

---

12 Deeper values are often implicated either consciously or subconsciously in management of a decision arc. Transparently understanding the influence of these deeper values on the decision maker's ability to act and react to both opportunities and threats is critical to increasing probabilities of success.

---

gan, promised to restore American strength on the global stage. He told Americans they could soon stand once again with their chests out and heads held high. Carter, in contrast, appeared weak. The images of crashed American helicopters strewn across the sand in a desert somewhere far away doomed his reelection.

For Obama, now ordering a helicopter-based operation utilizing US Special Forces in a desert far away, it felt like an eerily similar precipice for another Democratic president.

The outcome of an operation like this, and the decision that precedes the go-ahead, turns on a million small variables involving hundreds or thousands of individuals. The difference between success and failure is often the preparation, intelligence-gathering, processes, discipline, communication, and governance of those involved. Unlike Carter's Operation Eagle Claw, Obama's Operation Neptune Spear is successful. Bin Laden is executed, and a trove of materials pertaining to Al-Qaeda is obtained. Some sense of justice is achieved in the execution of a man who had orchestrated the murder of thousands of innocents. The operation helps salve a deep wound in the American psyche. Obama's political future rises. Americans feel powerful. Six months later, he is elected to a second term. This is his reward.

Tonight, Brooks and her colleagues in the White House Situation Room drop effortlessly into their operational modes, drawing on decades of experience. They begin to initiate the practiced routines and processes to effectively manage a million small variables that turn during moments like this.

Their mission has three parts. First, understand the facts on the ground in Paris, including only what is known and verifiable, and defining with clarity the scope of the unknown. Second, muster the US national security apparatus to gather information and monitor for coordinated attacks against the United States, whether at home or abroad. Third, prepare the fact pattern that will be presented to the president and his advisers for their interpretation and decision.

In this moment, their job is to turn an extraordinary situation into the ordinary.

PARIS

Friday, November 13, 2015, 9:36 p.m. CET (3:36 p.m. ET)

Another black SEAT sedan navigates the eleventh arrondissement. It pulls to a stop in front of 92 Rue de Charonne. Two gunmen jump out. They fire assault weapons into the diners at La Belle Équipe. The gunfire continues for three minutes before they get back into their car and flee.[181]

The front terrace is left a mangle of people, the dead and the alive. It is eerily quiet. No one cries. This darkened street of Paris is illuminated only by the yellow streetlights and small votives on café tables.

The silence ends when someone screams in horror. Nineteen dead and nine critically injured lie strewn on the sidewalk.

Among the dead are a waitress from a nearby restaurant and her sister. The sisters were French-Tunisian. They were Muslim. They were celebrating. Houda Saadi is killed on her birthday by another Muslim.[182]

The owner of La Belle Équipe survives.[183] He is Jewish. His wife, a Muslim, is killed.

The Islamic terrorists sought to send a message in their acts of wrath and hate. The reality is that the children of Abraham—Muslims, Jews, and Christians alike—all lie still and breathless on the cold sidewalk.

The terrorists' message has no meaning.

WASHINGTON, DC

Friday, November 13, 2015, 3:38 p.m. ET (9:38 p.m. CET)

In moments like this, the players have the perverse incentive to use the present facts and circumstances to gain their own advantage. They rush to conclusions and actions.

However, as President John F. Kennedy came to realize in

the wake of the 1961 Bay of Pigs fiasco, it is a mistake to run the calculus before you know the truth of realities on the ground. False assumptions, colored by the influence of those actors racing to seize upon a perceived opportunity, bias the observations. A game plan built upon a false foundation will fail.

These early moments in the unfolding crisis in Paris are squarely within the purview of the White House Situation

---

13 Enterprises that intentionally develop their institutional capability for exceptional judgment in a myriad of situational contexts gain significant advantage over both short and long decision arcs.

Room. Brooks, the handful of colleagues who staff the desks in the control room, and the men and women scattered in US operations centers around the world, begin extricating fact from the murky haze of confusion. They seek to ascertain facts that are unvarnished, without undue influence, without distortion, and without regard to the political theater, which will no doubt ensue in the hours, days, and weeks ahead.

PARIS
Friday, November 13, 2015, 9:40 p.m. CET (3:40 p.m. ET)

The simple café sits in the eleventh arrondissement. It pays homage to Voltaire.

Voltaire was one of the world's literary greats who clashed with the times in which he was born by advancing radicalized notions of civil liberties, free speech, free thinking, and the separation of church and state. His ideas were at the foundation of the Enlightenment, creating the philosophical underpinnings for the next great awakening in Western culture and society.

His ideas shaped young men of privilege to become the leaders of a distant colony across the Atlantic that would soon seek their own rebellion from the establishment. These were the men who would become known as the Founding Fathers of a new nation, built on a constitutional democracy that talked of civil liberties for all men, free speech, the virtues of free thinking, and a state free from church dogma.

This simple café is known as Comptoir Voltaire, or Voltaire's Counter, with chairs under its red awning for patrons to enjoy coffee, a croissant, and a cigarette, watching the world on the sidewalks of the arrondissement before them.

A man sits down at one of the small tables and studies the menu. He orders. As the waiter turns, the seated man detonates the homemade explosives-laden vest he wears under his coat. He kills himself and critically injures fifteen others who sit nearby.

Two kilometers to the north but also along the Boulevard Voltaire, American band Eagles of Death Metal sings "Kiss the Devil" to a sold-out audience of fifteen hundred people at the legendary Bataclan theater. At 9:42 p.m., a young man texts another, *"On est parti en commence"* (or "We have left and are commencing").[184] Three attackers enter the Bataclan with Zastava M70 assault rifles, the standard-issue weapon of the Yugoslav People's Army since the 1970s.[185] They wear suicide vests. They scream, "Allahu Akbar!," (or "God is great!") and open fire on the concertgoers.[186] Their fire is directed into the masses. They are practiced in the skill of one shooter firing while another replaces their empty clips with full ones. Several terrorists make it to the second level of the theater, giving them a vantage point. They shoot concertgoers huddled in front of the stage and those scrambling toward an exit to its left.

The bodies pile up on the floor. Some people lie alive among the dead, pretending they, too, are dead. One of the shooters reportedly yells that their actions are retribution for France's actions in Syria. After twenty minutes of firing, the terrorists take the remaining concertgoers hostage. Over the next two hours, the terrorists walk among those on the floor, kicking bodies, shooting those who are still alive or feigning death. Ninety lie dead. Another ninety-nine are critically injured.

Hollande declares a state of emergency. Over the next six days, police will conduct 412 warrantless searches.

The civil liberties of the French, freed by the philosophies of the Enlightenment and Voltaire's work, are suspended while terror roams the streets bearing his name.[187]

WASHINGTON, DC

Friday, November 13, 2015, 3:43 p.m. ET (9:43 p.m. CET)

Each morning, the president of the United States receives the Morning Book.[188] This book distills the critical happenings around the world from the past twenty-four hours. Naturally, within this briefing is a never-ending narrative pertaining to the continuing Middle Eastern conflicts and the stream of radical Islamists that spawn from them.

Obama's strategy is to contain their threats, sealing the terrorists into their warren, using drone strikes to destabilize their supply lines, executing their leadership, authorizing targeted military strikes when necessary, and using diplomatic wrangling to urge other countries to sort at their borders any terrorists who might sneak through with the true refugees and victims of these catastrophes.

Like the French and the national security experts, Obama's strategy may also be premised upon the belief that the terrorist cells that spring up under the umbrella of ISIS are not that sophisticated. The belief is that these cells could and would cause harm, but in the overall scheme, their threat to US national security is small. This calculus is harsh. It presumes an innocent life or two will be taken from time to time. It also presumes the threat of mass casualties on the scale of 9/11 is low. Many national security analysts and policymakers operate on an assumption at this time that if there were an attack, it would be by a lone wolf.[189] Their threat assessment assumes the highest-probability scenarios will be by a single individual rather than through a coordinated attack. They assess ISIS is still junior varsity.

As Brooks monitors the incoming information from Paris, every few minutes, a new attack is revealed. It is clear the assumptions are wrong. This is, in fact, a sophisticated, coordinated attack on the soil of a Western democracy.[190] Someone out there in the shadows has made varsity.[191]

The sixteen agencies that feed into the White House Situation Room immediately begin looking for patterns in the attacks that will help reveal who the attackers are, their motivations, their capabilities, and where they might strike next as part of their game plan.

Obama and his team now must react quickly and decisively if any dimension of the unfolding attacks targets America or Americans. They must also defend a purposeful strategy of containment when the blood on the streets of Paris shows its failings.

PARIS

Friday, November 13, 2015, 9:53 p.m. CET (3:53 p.m. ET)

At Stade de France, play continues between France and Germany. The crowd is gradually becoming aware of the threat outside. News alerts, texts, and calls from loved ones begin breaking through the typically spotty cellular coverage inside the stadium.[192]

Another explosion is heard. It is again toward the southeast corner of the stadium but seems a bit farther in the distance.

Another bomber has exploded himself. He, too, wore a matching homemade vest of TATP. He detonated himself near a McDonald's about four hundred meters outside the stadium.

He dies alone. His mission is a failure.

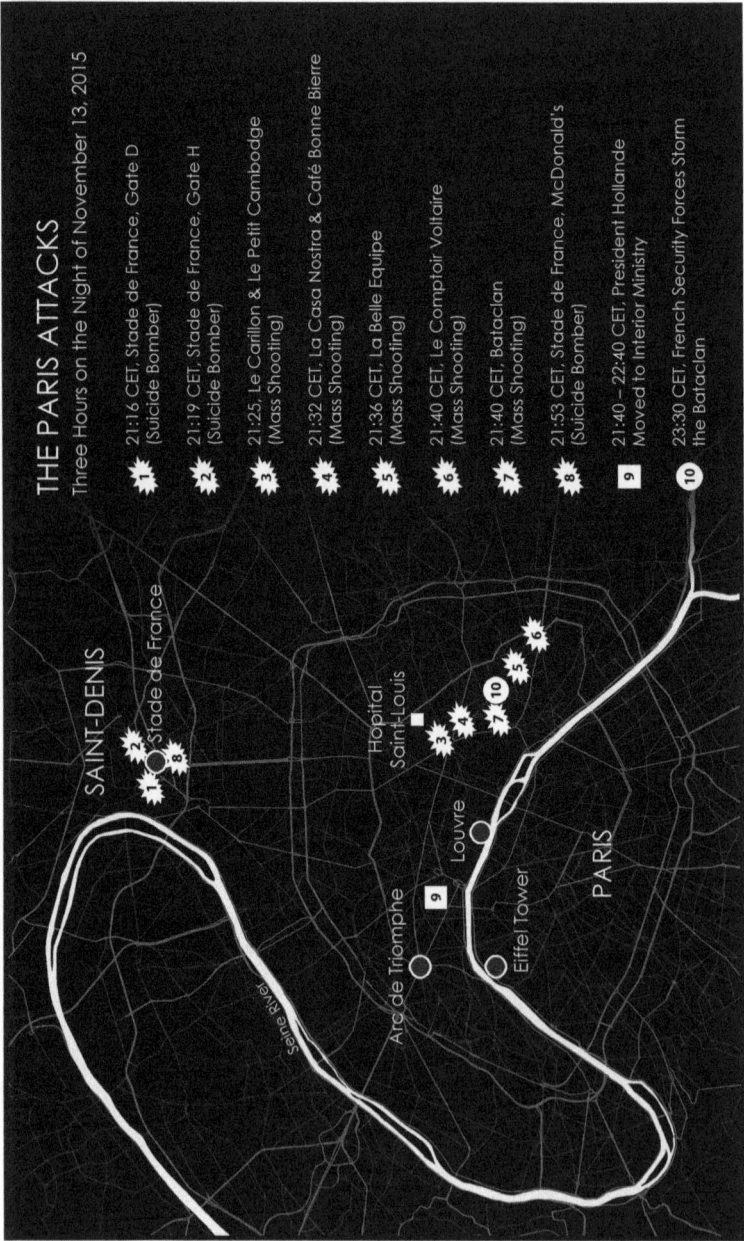

THE PARIS ATTACKS
Three Hours on the Night of November 13, 2015

1. 21:16 CET, Stade de France, Gate D (Suicide Bomber)
2. 21:19 CET, Stade de France, Gate H (Suicide Bomber)
3. 21:25, Le Carillon & Le Petit Cambodge (Mass Shooting)
4. 21:32 CET, La Casa Nostra & Café Bonne Bierre (Mass Shooting)
5. 21:36 CET, La Belle Equipe (Mass Shooting)
6. 21:40 CET, Le Comptoir Voltaire (Mass Shooting)
7. 21:40 CET, Bataclan (Mass Shooting)
8. 21:53 CET, Stade de France, McDonald's (Suicide Bomber)
9. 21:40 – 22:40 CET, President Hollande Moved to Interior Ministry
10. 23:30 CET, French Security Forces Storm the Bataclan

WASHINGTON, DC

Friday, November 13, 2015, 4:00 p.m. ET (10:00 p.m. CET)

Three suicide bombers have killed themselves over a twenty-three-minute period just outside the Paris stadium. Small teams of terrorists have moved through the city, killing dozens at restaurants. A concert hall has become a kill zone. Another kill zone could unfold among the eighty thousand inside the fences of the stadium. A hostage situation appears to be unfolding at the Bataclan.

It is no longer a quiet Friday afternoon in the White House Situation Room. The US national security apparatus is now fully stood up. It took less than ten minutes. Knowing the process, having well-developed communications channels, knowing the rhythms and cadences of a team in motion, and moving with speed and purpose positions the nation to react and respond quickly if necessary.

Intelligence analysts scramble. Airports and carriers scan for suspicious activities. Cities bolster their police at high-profile, potentially high-statement locations.

This is not an isolated incident by terrorists but instead a purpose-built game plan by an unseen enemy. Who is this? Where will they strike next? Where have they set their traps? What can we not see?

If the analysts are successful, Americans in New York, Miami, and Los Angeles will likely never know. Victories in this game are rarely celebrated. Those whose careers are in these fields do so to serve. They believe in the mission. They check their egos at the door. They will never be on the front page of *The New York Times*.

If they fail, however, the war on terror will ratchet to the next higher level. Obama's hand will be forced. His quiet maneuvering with drones, strike forces moving under the cover of darkness, and diplomatic cajoling will not quell the desire for revenge at home. He will then have to hunt for the kind of bloody trophies that can be held high in the air to appease the masses if the targets become American.

Obama's national security team begins filtering in from their offices in the Old Executive Office Building, along with leaders from the Pentagon, the State Department, intelligence agencies, and the Department of Homeland Security.

As Brooks and her team focus wholly on the "what," those assembling in the White House Situation Room begin preparing for "What now?" The recipe is simple but hard to execute. The pressure is immense. The opportunity is significant. The risks are extraordinary. More people will die somewhere, somehow—no doubt. Political futures can be made or lost in this moment.

Yet there is a discipline: First, get the facts right.[193] Then, give these facts meaning. Then, and only then, act.

PARIS

Friday, November 13, 2015, 10:55 p.m. CET (4:55 p.m. ET)

The referee blows his whistle to signal the end of play. The crowd cheers in victory. France defeats Germany 2–0. The announcer instructs guests to avoid certain gates when departing, stating simply that there has been an incident outside. Instead, thousands gather on the green grass of the playing field. As they learn of the carnage unfolding outside, they hug one another.

During the course of play, Hollande has been rushed to the interior ministry at the center of Paris to consult with his own national security and law enforcement teams. He closes the borders and increases security.

Paris is now littered with multiple crime scenes. Roads are jammed with first responders. Coordination of the response and the investigation is poor. Each crime scene is managed independently, making it harder to share evidence and hindering the ability to identify those patterns that might foretell what comes next in the game plan.[194]

The fans calmly exit the stadium singing "La Marseillaise," the French national anthem, letting it echo off the concrete halls.

Aux armes, citoyens!	*To arms, citizens!*
Formez vos bataillons,	*Form your battalions,*
Marchons, marchons!	*Let us march, let us march!*
Qu'un sang impur	*That their impure blood*
Abreuve nos sillons.	*Should water our fields.*

Across town, Hollande promises the French people that the response to the attacks will be merciless.[195] He will give them bloodied trophies as evidence of France's power and resolve. The rhetoric matches the moment.

The German team spends the night sleeping in the stadium on makeshift mattresses, unable to return to their hotel because of bomb threats. The French players stay with them.[196] The young French and German players who once would have otherwise warred upon one another now join together in solidarity.

Police amass outside the Bataclan theater. Hundreds of hostages are inside.

WASHINGTON, DC

Friday, November 13, 2015, 5:57 p.m. ET (11:57 p.m. CET)

Obama appears before the assembled reporters in the White House Press Room. He has just been briefed by his top counterterrorism adviser. He looks tired.

"I just want to make a few brief comments about the attacks across Paris tonight," he says. Obama comforts Americans and shows solidarity with the French people.[197] But he is cautious. He wants to know more. He is waiting for more of the fact pattern to emerge from the fog. He is not in a rush to make a decision or to act, at least it would appear.

There are embedded formulas within public statements like the one Obama was about to make. They reveal clues about those variables that precede the go/no-go decision that awaits. It is a practiced art at the highest echelons of politics and business to craft statements like this. Each sentence is programmed so that it can be plucked out as a sound bite on the news without context. The draftsman looks for the sweet spot that best launches the arc of the narrative, which will play out over the weekend, while averting it from being hijacked to serve someone else's agenda. The words themselves are carefully selected to elicit the right cognitive and emotional triggers that get cycled through FOX News, MSNBC, Twitter, and Facebook, shaping public sentiment for the days or months ahead.

Beyond the sentences, sound bites, and words, however, is the structure upon which the variables are hung.[198] This structure often reveals where the decision maker is on their own personal journey toward a likely go/no-go decision.

Across the Atlantic at this moment, Hollande is crafting his own narrative for the tribe of French people. They feel hurt, victimized, and vulnerable. They desire revenge. He needs to show a father's strength of caring for the French people as they cry and as they bleed. Yet this is not all he needs to do. He will also need to show the rising energy of a warrior preparing for war. *That their impure blood should water our fields.*

Before leaving the podium, Obama states, "It appears that there may still be live activity and dangers that are taking place as we speak."

Brooks and her team continue to orchestrate the facts, coordinating a vast network that is monitoring the events.[199] They look for patterns, talking through their channels with the French, working to keep Americans safe, and, no doubt, beginning to prepare for what will happen next, for there certainly will be a go decision.

Obama will exercise his judgment on the best path forward soon.

PARIS

Saturday, November 14, 2015, 12:20 a.m. CET
(Friday, November 13, 2015, 6:20 p.m. ET)

Men in black fatigues, black helmets with clear face shields, and black baklavas covering everything but their eyes gather in small teams around the perimeter of the Bataclan theater. They strap black vests around their torsos. Their energy rises. They are warriors preparing for an attack.

The French police know they face men inside also dressed in black and also wearing vests. Their vests, however, will not protect them from the bullets. The terrorists' vests will be laden with explosives that will send them into the mysteries of the afterlife, which they have been promised will be glorious but which everyone fears could be nothing at all. A dozen hostages remain inside the theater. Their fate is tied to whatever random moment lies ahead.

The order comes in. It is a go. French police storm the Bataclan. Once inside, a police officer fires at the torso of one of the men. His vest explodes in a sudden clap of fire, sending the man to whatever eternal fate awaits. The other two attackers detonate their own vests, quickly joining him. Twelve hostages survive.[200]

In the span of three darkened hours, 130 people are killed. Another 494 people are wounded, 99 critically.

The attacks are the worst acts of violence on French soil since the atrocities of WWII.

Deeper Codes.
Common Patterns.

Decision Arcs

There was a rhythm to my work with Peter D. Robinson, the parliamentarian and strategist. I would walk to the office early in the morning, inevitably spoiling a crisp white shirt with sweat from Washington, DC's oppressive humidity; scan the newspapers and regulatory reports looking for overnight developments, leaks, and gossip; and then grab a cab, most likely driven by an émigré from Africa or the Middle East. I'd strike up a conversation to learn their stories, wondering how they had made it to the United States and whether they were refugees from war, famine, or poverty, or perhaps were once guilty—a despot now tucked away by an intelligence agency in a nondescript apartment in the northern Virginia suburbs in exchange for a sin committed in a proxy war in some dirty capital most Americans could not find on a map.

Once on Capitol Hill, I would pass through security quickly to observe the wheels of democracy grind slowly. For the six decades prior to my arrival, Democrats had largely controlled both chambers. As the majority party, they set the rules for debate. Some of the rules were overt. Far more were exercised by fiat or discretion. Either way, by controlling the rules, the majority played overlord in the brutal competition among ideas, money, and power that underpins the democratic process. It was their privilege. It is a cardinal rule.

My purpose was to understand how these decisions would be shaped, made, or killed in the competition.

The DC summers spoiled white shirts because the swamp the city was built upon was drained to become the epicenter of the US government. It is no less hot or humid today than it was then. It is still a swamp, but one in which ideas continuously bubble and gurgle in a primordial goo. For some nascent ideas, the cells will successfully divide. Some will grow fins. Some will grow legs. Some will crawl up on the bank. Some will walk. Some will run. Those very few that do gain life, withstanding the treachery of their predators or the infirmities of a new strain poorly conceived, are deemed worthy by the overlords of entering more structured debate. They may percolate up through the committee hearings and the public relations campaigns, only then to possibly mature into something sufficiently well developed to begin further ascendance on the Darwinian path that shapes the American experience.

From here, the threats only become more powerful. Congressional staffs act as gatekeepers for what boils up for formal consideration. Senators and representatives of import will quietly control what ideas they deem worthy of consideration by the larger body. Those deemed unworthy are tamped down or abandoned. If the creature continues to advance sufficiently, the rules committees will set formal rules for the forthcoming larger body's debate. The parliamentarian's office will seek to make sure all is done in accordance with established rules and the arcane precedents of the House of Representatives or Senate where, respectively, Robinson had worked and would later work after my time with him. Outside the halls, pollsters will test public sentiment with their divining rods, whispering into the ears of their paying benefactors as to when to elevate a narrative in the public's mind or to bury it. Billions in private monies will be raised and spent by entrenched interests through advertising, public relations, and political campaigns, either to prop up or desecrate the emergent idea. It is war. Blood and carnage will be left everywhere. In the end, most ideas will be returned to the primordial goo to compost.

My job was to catch sight of whatever singular strain might be emerging from the mass. I was hunting for the viable contenders beginning to separate from all others. The few might make it fully through the gauntlet. They would be the ones from which the spoils of power and money would be bestowed, if only they could survive.

What I learned is that deciphering the living from the compostable was nearly always determined by asking less about the merit of an idea or policy—for if this were the criteria, there would be many viable ideas that could emerge fully erect, walk, and then run. Instead, I could better dis-

---

14 The deeper layers of the dynamics affecting the course of the decision arc must be drawn out and decoded.

---

cern those that ultimately wrangled through the treacherous gauntlet by asking several more fundamental questions:

How did we get here?
Who decides now?
What is the process and the pressures
that will shape the decision
going forward?

I would return to my office on Connecticut Avenue and sit with Robinson. He would quietly survey the decision arcs unfolding

15 Decoding how a decision arc will unfold increases the probability of successfully exercising judgment at crucible moments.

to anticipate how the game would develop, how the players would behave in their crucible moments, and, ultimately, how the spoils would be allocated to the victors and taken from the losers. We then went to work. Success would be found in understanding the unfolding arcs of the decisions and the forces shaping their path forward.

Energies within the Arc

Metaphorically speaking, there are parallels to how a decision arc moves and how the stone in the sport of curling moves. In this sweet and beautiful sport, one of those events that reminds us every four years during the Olympics of how Canadians and Norwegians spend their idle time, a thrower gracefully slides across the ice in a low lunge similar to the yoga pose Anjaneyasana. Toward the end of this slide, the player gently nudges a curling stone along its path. The stone looks somewhat like Grandma's teapot made of granite with a handle mounted on top. It glides toward a bull's-eye painted below the icy surface. The objective is to get closest to the centermost circle of the bull's-eye—or, if it is already occupied, to knock out an opponent's favorably resting stone. The sport is at once elegant and nasty.

To my inexpert mind, the game of curling is won or lost based on the aggregate effect of two offensive actions. The first action is, of course, setting the stone on its initial course across the ice with the right amount of force supplied by the first player on the three-person team. The second action comes from the team's other two members, who race out in front of the gliding stone, rubbing furiously at the ice in front of it. Collectively, the players yell to one another staccato commands with such force and volume that it brings back the

16 The decision arc will shift in response to both powerful and subtle forces seeking to change its course.

adolescent trauma of my father yelling profanities as I backed a gooseneck trailer up to a crooked gate in the dark.

The secret to the game seems to lie in creating enough heat on the surface of the ice to create a wet surface, reducing friction during the glide while affecting the force and rotation of the stone to bend its trajectory to a more ideal landing spot. The theoretical precepts of these physics, however, are hotly debated by those same Canadians and Norwegians.

Decision arcs work the same way, at least metaphorically. There is a natural trajectory that has already been put into motion. We inherit this first dimension of the decision arc. This inertia is extremely powerful.

17 A decision arc will have an inherited path that is fueled by inertia. Its future path is determined by the influences upon it, including how the actors exercise their judgment in seeking to direct it.

Then we go to work trying to influence the continuation of the trajectory. The goal is to increase the probability of our success by shaping the arc taken by the stone. We rub vigorously at the ice. Profanity is permitted.

Living Organisms

Decision arcs behave like living organisms. Each is a unique species, adapted and evolved to meet the requirements of their environment. Each operates on deeper codes that dictate their

---

18 Decision arcs behave like living organisms, each with their own patterns, proclivities, aptitudes, and inadequacies.

---

function and behavior. Each has a personality. Each courses through the realities of their environments, their situational contexts, seeking to be no one's prey and to emerge alive.

Trigger Points

To illustrate the forces at work upon the path of a decision arc, shaping it, separating those arcs that survive, those that thrive, and those that now must end, consider that fateful night in Paris as people lie dead and wounded, the crying, the scared, and the silent standing witness to the unfolding atrocities.

Obama inherited from George W. Bush the decision arc of the long-unfolding Global War on Terror. Whether that arc was improving or failing under Obama's stewardship was the subject of heated debate. The attacks on an otherwise ordinary Friday night in Paris may prove to be a trigger point along the arc.[201] Trigger points—sudden, dramatic inflection

---

19 Trigger points along the decision arc create the immediate necessity or potential opportunity to change its course.

---

points within the situational context that change the natural flow of the decision arc—create the opportunity for others to shift, impede, or transform the unfolding arc in their favor.

Consider the arc of Obama's Middle East strategy. It was premised upon two fundamental pillars, both of which were strongly supported by public opinion. First, he sought to extricate the United States from unpopular wars that had run for too long. Second, he sought to both destabilize and contain an elusive enemy.

Obama's challenge was demonstrating that he was serving both pillars well. In managing the arc, he would not have the benefit of visually stunning images of power and victory that

---

[20] There are layers within the decision arc. Some of the layers within the arc will be known and visible. Others hide. Some are hidden.

---

his predecessors possessed. There would be no photos of massive mobilizations of troops on their way to another war, as there had been with the Persian Gulf War, Afghanistan, or the Second Gulf War. There would be no video of a city being lit up in a "shock and awe" campaign, as there had been with the 2003 bombing of Baghdad. There would be no images of a statue being torn down, as there had been with Saddam Hussein. Obama faced a limitation in how he managed the unfolding arc. He had little meat that he could throw to the lions in the arena to delight the gathered masses. Displays of power and force would be less overt. He would have to work on a more subtle, more discreet basis to shape the arc in a manner that both defended American interests and his political capital. While serving many competing interests, he would have to be deft in how he swept the ice, carefully stewarding the arc in this moment. The truth be told, Obama had in fact exercised tremendous American power since he had assumed the inherited arc. He was just doing so through much quieter and darker methods.

Over the course of his presidency, Obama launched ten times more drone attacks on the infrastructure and leadership of terrorist organizations than had the prior Bush administration. The United States flew nearly eight thousand sorties over the Middle East during Obama's administration, representing some 78 percent of all sorties flown by coalition forces.[202] He deployed special forces for precision attacks, exploiting the United States' asymmetric advantage in executing rapid, stealthy missions at night using professional war fighters, including the action that led to bin Laden's assassination. Intelligence gathering, including through global telecommunications networks, vastly increased, at times pushing the limits of constitutionality, testing a former constitutional law professor's ability to balance enlightened civil liberties such as those tracing back to Voltaire against the realities of fighting a new enemy, one that could blend in with civilian populations, cross borders, and use modern, encrypted communications to manage what were increasingly global networks composed of small cells of radicalized terrorists, like those that seemed to be terrifying Paris in this moment.

In the wake of the unfolding attacks in Paris, with the visuals of lifeless bodies strewn in the streets and pulsing blue-and-red lights in the night illuminating Paris's first responders racing to the next attack, it would be easy for those with something to gain by redirecting Obama's arc—Republican or Democrat—to make the case that he was failing. They sought their own trophies. Perhaps they would advocate for the common good. Or perhaps they would try to garner a few more points in their polls or take a few away from Obama. Perhaps they would use the event to activate their bases, getting them more agitated and vocal, enough to send campaign donations. Regardless, Obama could be certain that within hours, maybe sooner, the Paris attacks would be used by others for their gain.

Trigger points like this will also reveal further clues about Obama's own calculus, his logic, his fears, his ability to tap

21 Trigger points reveal how a leader acts and reacts to pressure and change.

into the emotions of a populace afraid, and the demands of being a rational global steward, as the American president is expected to be. This trigger point will increase the intensity placed on his decision-making. This pressure could affect his immediate reaction, his own emotions, and his gut-level response. It could provoke a shift in his Middle East strategy, forcing him to give more red meat to the agitated masses by visibly demonstrating the power of the United States through a force buildup in the region once again. It could reshape the narrative in the upcoming presidential election. Better yet, for the opportunists, the intensity and pressure could force him to make a mistake, reveal a secret, or commit a gaffe. Errors alone can create the opportunity for others to shift the arc.

22 Critics and opportunists will use trigger points to shift, impede, or transform the course of the decision arc in their favor.

For Republicans, the calculus was simple.[203] The tragedy would set off a new news cycle. They would attack. Republicans would take to the airwaves in the coming hours and days, using the Paris attacks to press the narrative that Obama's Middle East strategy was a failure. While they spoke, video would scroll onscreen showing the carnage of Paris, with bodies strewn on the terraces of Le Petit Cambodge and Le Belle Équipe, and the soccer game patrons locked inside the stadium to protect them from the evil outside. They would tap into the primal emotions of fear, anger, and a desire for retribution against those who can commit such irrational, cruel acts and their modern sophistication to do so. While Obama, known colloquially as "No Drama Obama," would predictably urge for calm and reason, Republicans would stoke the flames, increase the pressure, and hope to knock Obama's stone from its arc.

On the other side of the aisle, Democrats also have something to gain. The primaries leading to a presidential election cycle are fully underway. A Democratic primary debate will occur a little more than twenty-four hours from now in Iowa. Hillary Clinton, Obama's former Secretary of State, may use the Paris attacks as an opportunity to take a more hawkish foreign policy stance, arguing for quick and aggressive retribution against ISIS targets in Syria and Iraq. No doubt, she will study her three-ring binders over the next twenty-four hours, running the calculus through her mind of whether to use this carnage to go tougher, herself feeding red meat to the lions and the roar of the assembled crowd, or hew toward a more moderated stance largely undifferentiated from Obama's at the risk of being portrayed as a woman too timid or weak to become the next president and inherit the long-running arc of the Global War on Terror.[204]

---

23 Trigger points can free or authorize an actor to set a new course for their own decision arc.

While the battle to win over domestic constituencies rages between Republicans and Democrats—enabled by traditional media and social media industries that live on the energy created by each new trigger point in public discourse—Obama's calculus must also factor in his global responsibilities. Within

24 Many thrive on the energy created by trigger points, finding vitality, relevance, and gain not in the resolution of conflict or confusion, but instead in its longevity and amplification. They revel in decisions that are deferred or made in error.

forty-eight hours, he will meet with the G20 economic summit leaders, including the leaders of Russia and Türkiye. Maintaining a global alliance united in the fight against terrorism will be integral to Obama's long-term success, and the Paris attacks provide him with an opportunity to further strengthen this alliance.

Something else might be at play in this meeting, however, which may represent a trigger point for changing the trajectory on yet another decision Obama must curate as part of his presidency: the United States' relationship with Russia. If navigated effectively, this meeting could provide a turning point in Obama's relationship with Russian president Vladimir Putin, whose playbook had seemed as simple as opposing anything advanced by the West. In the current situational context, Russia and the United States seem to share a position in rooting out terrorist cells in Syria. Russia has just suffered its own tragic losses. Just several weeks before, roughly two hundred Russians died when terrorists downed a Metrojet flight in retribution for Russia's actions in Syria. Obama and Putin might be able to find common ground at last on at least one issue. Obama himself may be able to use this trigger point as his opportunity to change the decision arc that stems from US-Russia relations.

Obama's possible paths forward are several. First, he can lock in and stay the course with his strategy. He will continue to launch air strikes on ISIS.[205] He can continue a highly selective bombing campaign, using precision strikes to take out pieces of the Syrian oil infrastructure, destabilizing it but never fully destroying it.[206] In effect, he is playing a high-stakes game of Jenga, pulling one piece out of the terrorists' stack at a time, causing harm, slowing progress, and destabilizing the structure but being careful to not cause it to fully collapse. With this strategy, he can retain hope that Syria's oil infrastructure can be returned to the Syrian people at some point to help finance the nation's rebuilding. He will strive to limit civilian casualties at all times, hoping to eliminate the bad actors from the population but not slip into the indiscriminate killing of innocents as a casualty of war. This is the moral high ground of modern war, and Obama seeks to maintain it. It is vastly different from that of terrorists and the Russians, whose playbooks embrace the indiscriminate and callous slaughter of civilians caught in the fray.[207] Obama can continue pinning terrorists in their desert confines, preventing their spread into Europe and America through weak borders in Türkiye. He will rope them in with sophisticated nets of eavesdropping and intelligence. He will stay the course and keep American ground troops out of Syria, except for the limited number of special forces there to help Kurdish minorities fight another enemy, the Assad regime itself.[208]

Or Obama could go for even bigger trophies. He could give his audience more blood, more revenge, and more overt symbols of American brute power on the global stage. This could be his moment to ratchet up America's demonstration of power and force, more similar to that exercised by his predecessor, Bush, who at a different time and within a different situational context had license from a unified American electorate to hunt for big trophies after the 9/11 terrorist attacks.

Back then, Americans wanted immediate justice and revenge for the Al-Qaeda attacks on US soil. It is the sort of demand from the electorate that gives license to the leader, much like President Hollande would be granted. He would be authorized, if not encouraged, to go hunt for the big, visible trophies that come from acts of revenge and justice. Hollande would in fact immediately take license, pitch his rhetoric higher, and tell the people of France that the nation would hunt down the "barbarians."[209] Obama's license would likely be less, as Americans had not been directly attacked in this instance. In further contrast, coming from a different value system and heritage, the terms of the license in Russia are written differently. Putin held a persistent license to be tough, if not draconian, in virtually all foreign affairs. The West is typically frustrated with this broad and persistent license, but given the present situational context, including the downing of the Metrojet airliner, the West would seek to use this instance of common victimization as an opportunity to find a shared purpose.

It is important in these moments to look for the clues that

---

25 When an actor sets a new course for the decision arc, all other players must reevaluate and potentially reestablish their positioning in the game.

---

indicate a player is seeking to reshape the course of the decision arc. One act in particular will signal if Obama is going big against the Islamic terrorists in Syria and Iraq.[210] If he authorizes the insertion of ground forces into Syria, it is a clear sign that he is dramatically changing his own decision arc in favor of a far more committed, aggressive stance. If he makes this move, all other players, from Republicans to Democrats, from the Europeans to Putin, will be forced to make a corresponding shift. Their strategies and narratives must reset to reflect the shifting path of the decision arc.[211]

Continual realignment is simply part of the ever-changing game.

The Force of Water

In addition to the trigger points that have the potential to dramatically influence a decision arc with a sudden event, a decision arc is under another continuous, more persistent force. It is subtle but just as powerful or perhaps even more so: *the force of water*.

The force of water is fluid and ever-changing, pressuring the path of the decision arc as the situational context shifts. As it changes, the force reveals further clues about the players, their strengths, their weaknesses, and the shifting rules of the game.

---

26 **The force of water is a fluid, ever-changing pressure on the decision arc created by an ever-shifting situational context.**

Imagine Timothy Geithner and the bank executives, each with their respective teams facing the threats and opportunities of the financial crisis, having marked out their individual positions along a river that is the decision arc unfolding. Each team stands as a cluster upon its mound or stack of stones in the current. Some clusters are a bit upstream, and some are a bit farther down, looking like fly-fishermen spread out in a

27 The ever-changing forces affecting the course of the decision arc reveal truths about the players, their positions, and their respective probabilities of success.

river. They are within eyesight of one another, far enough to retain their space, but close enough to see who is getting a bite and who is not. A storm is mounting. The clouds are darkening, turning from gray to black. The rain begins as a trickle. The water rises subtly. The rain starts to fall a bit faster. The drops grow bigger. The water runs higher, becoming more powerful and more volatile. The skies become angrier. A deluge unfolds. The force of the water is now violent, tearing at everything in its path.

In 2008, the rising force of water was the liquidity crisis that transformed quickly from a trickle to a rage. Geithner had

28 By monitoring the ebbs and flows unfolding within a decision arc and the players' reactions to it—and by profiling their respective decision archetypes—a player can better identify targets of opportunity and formulate their own strategy.

built his dam in the river, stating it was impermeable, meaning taxpayers would not be asked to bail out the banks. He posited that his dam could not be broken. The working groups of bank executives gathered on their own high points along the river to watch. They bore witness to whether his dam could hold against the growing pressure. They tested him as a player.

The objective of the game, of course, is to withstand the volatile force of the water, scramble to shore up your own position when necessary, and watch to see who is failing fastest and who will last longest. Perhaps you'll build alliances when there is shared gain, send out a plea for help when vulnerable, or simply watch as a peer slips away.

As the water increased in its volatility, the banks Geithner called in were gauging how each fared against the rage. They discovered their relative positions were shifting. The waters lay waste to some. Others were growing stronger.

The force of the water dissolves arguments and positions until the truth is revealed, free of obfuscations, varnish, spin, and artificial or false foundations. Decision-making processes,

---

29 Many enterprises and individuals seek to shield the inner workings of their decision archetypes. Change and pressure, however, often reveal those inner workings, both in ways that are known and unknown to the player.

---

dependencies, blind spots, and motivations become more transparent. Who is to be trusted and the values to be held most tightly become known, including what a player honors most and what they are willing to sacrifice. The force of the water does not always yield what is equitable, fair, or right—only the truth about the player, their position, and their probability of succeeding or surviving from this point forward. As the water wipes away all but the truth, our ability to forecast the path of a decision arc going forward improves.

Misalignment

Joseph Cassano was the son of a Brooklyn cop. He went to Brooklyn College, studying political science. After graduating, he spent eighteen months in Nebraska as an AmeriCorps VISTA volunteer on a Native American reservation.[212] It was an unlikely beginning for those who typically ascend to the highest ranks of finance and are more ordinarily in possession of degrees from prestigious universities and well-connected families able to open doors for their sons and daughters.

When he returned home, he began his career in finance as a clerk in the back office of First Boston. He spent the days cutting checks for principal and interest payments due counterparties. After several years, he joined a new unit within First Boston that traded interest-rate swaps, novel new instruments in the fledgling field of financial derivatives. He subsequently joined Drexel Burnham Lambert, the firm made infamous by Michael Milken, the financial innovator later known as the "junk bond king." (Milken would become a felon and pardoned by President Donald Trump in 2020.)[213]

Cassano developed his own reputation while working his way up the ladder at Drexel. He was a workhorse.[214] He gave everything to his job, outworking his colleagues.[215] He was flawless in the execution of trades. His career also gravitated toward those segments of the financial markets most at the cutting edge. In 1987, he had the opportunity to push into the next frontier of financial innovation. A small group of mathematicians within Drexel envisioned new cracks of light where they suspected they could earn outsize financial rewards. Cassano, the operations guy, was asked to join the fledgling team.

To execute their vision, the mathematicians needed two assets not available at Drexel:[216] they needed a backer with a massive balance sheet, and that backer needed an AAA rating. AIG was one of only several companies in the world that possessed both. A Wall Street lawyer introduced the group to Hank Greenberg at AIG. Greenberg, also known as an innovator, albeit in the insurance markets rather than in exotics like derivatives, agreed to bring the group into AIG as a new subsidiary. He had two demands. First, AIG and FP would split the profits they created with AIG. Greenberg would take 65 percent, and the new brainiacs would keep 35 percent. Second, if FP did anything that jeopardized AIG's AAA rating, Greenberg promised to go after them "with pitchforks."[217]

AIG would keep close tabs on the experimentations of FP but allowed it to operate differently from the insurance company. This would not be another Wall Street operation filled with traders and investment bankers swaggering around the room with overbearing machismo. Instead, FP would be populated by geeky mathematicians. They were the *quants*, as they are known on Wall Street.[218] Instead of organizing themselves in chain-of-command-style hierarchies common in large financial institutions like AIG or investment banks, they would organize themselves more fluidly, like a think tank or an academic department,[219] with all the smart folks brainstorming ideas, testing their arguments, and pushing one another to be more bold, more creative, and smarter, all the while checking one another's work for errors.[220] Instead of trying to build a larger and larger machine that could process more trades or underwrite more insurance, taking a tiny sliver of profit from massive amounts of capital (the model embraced by most of Wall Street), these brainiacs searched out isolated problems to be fixed, like the bottlenecks or inefficiencies of regulatory

---

30 Studying a competitor's enterprise archetype will reveal their ability to evolve, adapt, attack, hide, or retreat.

---

impediments or outdated risk models that kept capital from flowing into otherwise economically valuable enterprises. In short, this group looked for problems others could not solve. They would then work months or even years to develop solutions, rendering iteration upon iteration of ways to navigate the complex intricacies of risk analysis, regulatory barriers, market inefficiencies, and legal structures to navigate the minefields those less capable could not.

In the first decade of its existence, the diligent and careful process of financial engineering might yield only one or two deals per year, but FP would be paid tens or hundreds of millions of dollars for solving the problems no one else could, from financing coal mining equipment in Appalachia to hedging currency risk across a basket of Asian credit card receivables. FP's business model was to find markets with asymmetric problems, solve those problems in highly creative ways, and do so while taking on little to no financial risk. FP would then maximize their harvest from the new market they had created up until the point when the copycats showed up—which, when someone finds a way to make money on Wall Street, the hordes behind them always do. In fact, the colloquial rule was that if you were still in the market when Bear Stearns showed up with their copycat offering, then you had been in the market too long.

FP's original business model was simple: Go into markets early where they could be the visionaries and innovators. Open up the market with their ideas and capabilities. Harvest outsized profits[221] because there was no competition. Then, when the other firms started to enter the market, driving down prices and oftentimes standards, move on in search of the next abstract and elusive problem and make a heap of money by solving that one, too. Rinse and repeat. FP was the very embodiment of the type of financial innovation that free-market disciples like Alan Greenspan and Greenberg both prophesized. This was in their DNA.

Cassano's journey with FP began in 1987 as its inaugural chief financial officer. In 1989, he was sent to London to grow the European operations. In 1994, he became FP's chief operating officer, retaining much of his CFO responsibilities but also taking on management of FP's transaction development group. Once again, his career was focusing on opportunities at the forward edge of finance, helping the smart guys execute their newest ideas. One of these was creating a new market for credit derivatives. The first small transactions were piloted around 1996, but then officially in 1998 with a small transaction led by J.P. Morgan.

In 2002, Cassano rose to become FP's chief executive officer, responsible for its diverse activities across North America, Asia, and Europe. By many measures, it was an astounding rise to the upper echelons of finance.

When Cassano took over as CEO of FP, he made it more like AIG's big machine. No longer would FP be a brainy think tank working to push the creative edge of financial innovation. Instead, it shifted to grinding out slivers of profit from massive, replicable deals, just like the insurance or trading businesses. FP also shifted from being a collaborative that worked at the fringe of the financial markets, where there was no competition in harvesting massive profits by fixing problems no one else could solve, to instead becoming a command-and-control enterprise, cooperating and competing with the likes of Goldman Sachs, Merrill Lynch, J.P. Morgan, Bear Stearns, and the monoline insurers. Instead of finding valuable strains of gold where there was no competition, FP shifted to panning for gold in the same stream with them.[222] The DNA was changed.

No longer was FP the quirky financial think tank out in the suburbs somewhere near Yale University. Instead, it was molded to fit Cassano's desired organizational form. No longer a collaborative with the brainiacs looking over one another's shoulders[223] to make sure errors were not being made or blind spots being overlooked, it was shaped into a hierarchical pyramid with a powerful boss at the top.[224] It began to look more like the or-

---

31 When the enterprise archetype is misaligned to the situational context it faces, it is weak and vulnerable.

---

ganizational form that underpinned Greenberg's empire. The chain of command was clear and simple. Communications were no longer omnidirectional, touching many different people with different perspectives, but instead became linear, flowing along well-established paths. Before, with FP's think tank structure, the greatest fear was making a mistake in problem-solving or risk analysis in the eyes of your peers. Now the greatest fear was reprisal from a screaming Cassano.[225] The FP enterprise architecture changed to fit the decision archetype of its leader.

Its enterprise architecture was misaligned with the challenges it would soon face.

Decision Archetypes

Leaders come to us possessing differing decision archetypes. Some of their archetype will be the product of their imprint. They are born with it. Some is learned. Much of it is shaped by their life experiences.

---

32 Each decision maker possesses predetermined decision archetypes they bring to the unfolding decision arc.

Decoding the archetype, including its underlying chemistry and influences, helps us understand how the leader will play the game before them. It reveals how they will perceive, react, and think as the conditions intensify or grow more uncertain. They calibrate how a leader aligns their fundamental priorities, including those that innately define their thought processes and actions.

---

33 Decoding the decision archetype reveals how a decision maker will perceive, react, and think under uncertain conditions and intensified pressure.

Then, when the leader is placed under strain or threat, the deeper codes will naturally percolate to the surface. The sunlight will reveal those who innately protect their own self-interest over all other interests. Their *I* will come first. Others will place a paramount interest in the fate of their tribe—that is, those they lead. Primacy is given to their *we*. Still others will defend a higher ideal, expressed as an *idea*, such as the common good of society, equity, or faith.

By extricating these codes, it is then possible to better foretell the decision maker's biases, patterns, logical structures, and the processes by which they will be compelled to

---

34 The deeper codes within the decision archetype tells us who a leader trusts, the language they will use, and what they will need from others.

---

make certain choices over others. These codes also enable us to forecast who they trust and distrust, the language they will use, and what they feel they need from others to be successful. It will shape what they perceive as a threat, and where they will find safety.

While being interviewed in 2010 by the government-appointed Financial Crisis Inquiry Commission investigating the underlying causes of the financial crisis, and long after Cassano had been forced out of AIG, Cassano's lawyer provided an extended opening statement to the commission's investigators. The lawyer focused his remarks on shaping how Cassano would be remembered.[226] It was an odd request. In many ways, however, it was predictable. Cassano's deepest psychological need in that moment was to serve his *I*.

Cassano had been relegated for the prior two years to

sitting in exile behind drawn drapes in his prestigious London home, at least when he was not dealing with an onslaught of depositions and legal investigations.[227] A man little known outside Wall Street, or perhaps even the narrow confines of the CDO market, was now known to the greater public as the "the man who crashed the world."[228] He had been vilified by the media, the financial industry, Congress, and various prosecutorial bodies.[229] It would not be hard to imagine his personal perception of identity being in shambles.

Cassano had amassed tremendous wealth over his career.[230] He did so by harvesting maximum rewards from his beautiful machine year over year. He took home $45 million in 2005 alone.[231] It was a long way from his humble beginnings as a boy in Brooklyn. He accomplished this crowning achievement by being an operational workhorse and a deft negotiator, but also by being a bully and a tyrant to those nearest him. It was clear to all who worked with him that Cassano worked in service of Cassano. His self-interest was paramount in the decisions he faced.

Cassano's deeper codes would have been known to those who knew him best on Wall Street. The other players in the game, those also wearing bomb-laden vests interwoven with red-and-black wires, would have profiled Cassano's archetype. In their own practiced arts, they would have known that when threatened, he would react in service to his own self-reward and self-identity. He would stake an intransigent position. He would be resistant to change and adaptation. He would seek to preserve his beautiful machine, and he would be slow-footed as the situational context shifted, the rules changed, and conditions worsened. They knew he would fight to the end rather than cede one inch in the calamity before him.

Cassano's challenge was that the exceptional strong dominance of his *I*-first orientation over other possible orientations made him a fighter of a singular dimension. He would get boxed in. He would not build escape hatches. He could not later tilt the rules of the game in his favor when they changed because his sensitivities were not attuned to sensing the shifts, nor activating new logical structures, communications approaches, language, or strategies more adept to the new game being played. He lacked the broader combat arsenal possessed by greater leaders better able to create asymmetric advantages in their moments of need, either by shifting their techniques to the realms of political gamesmanship, by currying regulatory favor, or by winning in the court of public opinion.

In the biggest fight of his life, Cassano's only endgame seems to have been the hope that the market would recover and the pain of the moment would resolve. Given the deeper codes within his decision archetype, it was the only endgame he could envision. If he tried to subsequently present himself as embracing a *we*-orientation, arguing that the problems of the crisis were systemic to the larger Wall Street or that he was always acting in service to the AIG tribe involving hundreds of thousands of employees, the perspective would feel

---

35 Strategies that attempt to leverage decision archetypes that are inauthentic to the leader will prove ineffective.

---

inauthentic. It would feel opportunistic. It would feel like an explanation retrofitted in the several years following the darkest days of the crisis as part of a legal and reputational defense. It would feel inconsistent with his being and reputation in the years and decades before, which had clearly placed the *I*-first orientation at the forefront of his decision archetype.

The *I*-first orientation was not exclusive to Cassano, however. It was exhibited by all of the players in the subprime crisis. It was on full display in the strategies and decisions made by each of the banks embroiled in the crisis. In fact, with this orientation, many actually profited from it, emerging stronger in the subsequent years. They avoided a *we*-based solution to the crisis during its darkest days. Their *I*-first strategy ultimately won.

---

36 You are being studied. They want to know how you think and how you will respond.

There are practiced arts that decipher the deeper codes of decision archetypes. In Robinson's office and in offices across Washington, DC, thousands of hours are spent dissecting the codes that shape or define the decision archetype of individual leaders, whether in Congress, the White House, numerous federal agencies, or foreign governments. It is also the domain of the intelligence agencies, who parse the psychology of foreign leaders, powerful interests, and terrorists, looking to anticipate how they will move next, reacting to threats in their immediate environments, or deferring their fight until another day.

---

37 Improve the mark on a player by profiling their decision archetype.

Similarly, my speculation is that there would have been long conversations inside Goldman Sachs anticipating how their executives thought Cassano and the other executives at AIG would react once the first capital call was triggered. Goldman Sachs knew Cassano. It likely had studied his codes, just as it would have studied Greenberg's before him and that

38 Studying decision archetypes is a practiced art among competitors.

of other powerful actors in the drama, including Geithner. They knew that when Cassano took the first punch, he would fight back. They knew that if they could jab, dance, stall, and survive the short battles along the way, they could win the long war—which they did.

Cassano, on the other hand, came to be known as "patient zero" in the larger systemic breakdown of the subprime crisis.[232] In fairness, the crisis was not his fault alone. The fault lay with the collective *we* involved in the trading of subprime instruments—that is, the thousands of executives and regulators who collectively turned a blind eye to the foibles and fallacies that underpinned the system, making them rich so long as the music still played. The injustice was that when the music stopped, many who had played in the game and shared responsibility for the systemic failure were allowed to continue playing on.[233]

Lineage

Cassano's rise in the AIG organization was not only attributable to his reputation as a workhorse.[234] He was also a voracious student. As he rose within AIG, he carefully studied the ways of Greenberg,[235] its legendary CEO often known in the corporate world as "Hank", a single-name moniker equivalent to pop culture's Elvis, Cher, or Madonna.

Hank's legend began early in New York when his father, a taxi driver, was killed in an accident.[236] His mother remarried, this time to a dairy farmer. Hank moved from the city to a farm in New York. At sixteen, lying about his age, he signed with the US Army and served in WWII. He stormed the beaches of Normandy on D-Day, fought across Europe, and, ten months later, helped liberate Dachau, a Nazi concentration camp. He returned home and studied to become a lawyer, then reentered the army to lead men in combat during the Korean War.

When he returned home for a second time, he decided he did not have the patience required to be a lawyer. Instead, he shifted paths, becoming an insurance executive. Over the course of the next thirty-four years, he expanded AIG to become a global empire with over $1 trillion in assets, operating in 130 countries with over one hundred thousand employees. The company developed a reputation for being a foremost innovator in the global insurance industry, able to open new markets, create new products, and consistently achieve solid earnings.[237] Hank positioned AIG within the insurance industry at the very tip of the spear of financial innovation.

Hank possessed a clear leadership archetype unto himself. He was a chieftain in every way. He built an empire, overseeing a multihued patchwork of corporate subsidiaries, each a distinct faction knit together within the larger tribe. He was a vi-

---

39 A decision archetype is like a fingerprint. Each is unique.

---

sionary, pushing the tribe ahead, stewarding its health, finding new areas of growth, and, when necessary, stepping down from the pedestal and into the trenches to lead when the moment called for it. He treated the business of underwriting insurance a lot like the exercise of leading men in combat. He demanded the loyalty of his lieutenants without reservation. He brokered the infighting, at times stoking it to promote competition, seeing which emerging leaders possessed the strength, stamina, and cunning to continue their ascents. He also calmed the fighting when it did not serve the larger purpose of AIG, which was wholly indistinguishable from his own. A career in AIG was based on Darwinian principles, with the stronger, most cunning, and at times most brutal lieutenants rising and the lesser ones sloughing off.[238] It is the ethos upon which empires, whether political or financial, are most often built.

The insurance business is based upon earning profits by assuming the risks of others. To win in this game, like in combat, the leader's greatest asset is acquiring and maintaining asymmetric advantage over the enemy. Hank ensured AIG's asymmetric advantage through a superior understanding of the market, including intelligence on its competition in various market segments; its relationships with regulators, foreign leaders, and other financial institutions, enabling it to tilt opportunities in its favor when necessary; a massive and pristinely kept balance sheet; and an AAA rating from the various ratings agencies. Then, true to a simple and fundamental law of free market capitalism, AIG's asymmetric advantage over its competition enabled it to create the leverage and power to harvest profit. If financial validation is the ultimate metric of Wall Street, which it is, then Hank was its darling. He predictably earned 15 percent profits year-over-year for shareholders during the course of his thirty-four years at the helm.

Hank ran a beautiful machine. He also knew that the greatest liability of a combatant in the risk game is one's poor judgment.

---

40 The greatest liability for a leader is poor judgment. The leader who makes poor decisions under pressure is a liability to themselves and everyone around them.

Consequently, Hank was a micromanager,[239] keenly aware of all aspects of his empire at any given time, challenging executives, poking and prodding to test their judgment in the moment, sorting the good ones from the bad.[240] When a mistake was made, Hank would immediately and personally jump on the problem, riding herd on the individual who had erred to fix it. He sensed trigger points and made sure to help manage through them so that AIG emerged intact rather than risk any festering that might foretell the beginning to an end.

At the time of the Asian financial crisis in the late 1990s, for example, Hank abruptly left an AIG leadership meeting in Dallas, Texas, and hopped aboard a private jet to Hong Kong to personally sit beside a young executive as they unwound a trade that had soured.[241] He was a four-star general at the helm of the army but would drive to the front and assume the firefight as a captain leading his men in battle when circumstances required. These stories fueled his legend. They became woven into the tribal lore of AIG. The lore united the vast number of AIG employees around the world with a common identity, purpose, and collective narrative for what it meant to be a part of this tribe.

Hank governed through a structure typical of history's powerful tribes, with pyramidical order to power and a paramount authority at the peak, which of course was him. There was a board of directors,[242] but they served more as a tribal council readied for consultation and to vet ideas and pathways forward. Hank was the ultimate arbiter of the major decisions, and he directed the executive team to implement his orders. Within the governance structure of Hank's tribal nation, there were circles of influence, bestowing rank and privilege based upon the achievements and favor of the executives. These circles emanated out from Hank, providing access to inner tiers of compensation, prestige, and power.[243] Those deemed most worthy gained access to a private company that had little purpose other than to own a major stake in the publicly traded AIG corporate entity and also created further incentive compensation for the most valued lieutenants.

Among global corporate heavyweights, this was an unusual structure for ownership and governance. Some described AIG as a public surrey but with a private fringe on top.[244] It was an essential element of Hank's governance model, enabling him to allocate power in the organization and use compensation as the lever for preserving the health of the AIG tribe.[245] He also used mechanisms like this to create an unbreakable bond between the managers and AIG. Significant portions of their wealth were placed into these compensation vehicles, inaccessible to them until they retired. They were bound to the tribe for life.

While Hank was chieftain, others characterized him as a son of a bitch. He played in the insurance business the same way he had led men in combat, where the difference between life and death comes down to how cunning you are, how creative you are, and, at times, how brutal you are. It requires diplomacy in certain moments, tilting the rules of the game in your favor, and in others, a willingness to engage in bloody battles involving blunt assault when required.

Cassano, the student, seems to have modeled significant portions of his own managerial approach to replicate what he saw in Greenberg. By contrast, however, he apparently overweighted one dimension in his leadership patterning: He relished being a son of a bitch. He was a tyrant and a bully.[246] He kept his lieutenants aboard his own team only through extraordinary compensation,[247] the one lever over which he retained exclusive control in the FP organization.[248] He was quick with the stick and used the carrot of compensation[249] to keep his reports on the team.[250] Unlike the sophisticated financial engineering created by FP, as a managerial technique, it was remarkably blunt.

In many ways, Cassano sought to mimic the leadership and the governance structures he saw Hank use successfully. He missed some important differences, though. Hank was a true chieftain, able to play different roles in different settings, all in greater service to the empire he had built.[251] Cassano was simply a tyrant. Cassano paced the floor of the London office, hyperaware of all the activities across Europe, North America, and Asia, communicating with each desk daily, sometimes hourly. He was frequently ruthless to his direct reports within FP, prone to emotional outbursts when someone had erred or

41 An admired decision archetype cannot simply be adopted from another person. It must be crafted from within an individual and represents the multihued influence of one's own psychological needs, values, skills, and experiences.

offended him, like Gene Park when he had identified significant market risk in FP's credit derivatives portfolio.

Like Hank, Cassano also made the business feel like combat. However, unlike the prior leadership at FP and perhaps unlike Hank, Cassano's source of strength was not secured by being the smartest guy in the room. Time and time again, for

42 The larger decision archetype of an enterprise that is merely a reflection of the individual leader's decision archetype is vulnerable as the situational context changes.

example, he blindly deferred to the models built by the analysts for the credit derivatives business,[252] seemingly oblivious to the fact that these evaluated only credit default risk while remaining ignorant of other forms of risk, such as valuation risk, liquidity risk,[253] or systemic risk.[254] These latter forms of risk, unaccounted for or misperceived, would in fact prove lethal in the end to FP and his career.

Cassano's authority stemmed from his capacity as an exceptional trader able to negotiate the finer point of arcane deals and, more primally, from his capacity to be the biggest son of a bitch in the room. What he lacked was Hank's ability to tilt whatever game he was playing in his favor. Hank had a diverse arsenal and could alternatively use power, financial advantage, regulatory arbitrage, or political favor to create asymmetric advantage, recast a battlefield, create new pathways for a victory, or enable an escape from the predicament ahead.

---

43 Gifted decision makers are able to align or adapt dimensions of their decision archetype to the unique situational context they presently face. Their decision archetype has dimension, variability, and adaptability, which can be configured to best respond to or manage any number of differing situational contexts.

Cassano's arsenal was singular. He was a trader and negotiator. He was an easy read and, most likely, an easy mark. In the moment when Goldman Sachs made an unprecedented capital call on FP of an extraordinary sum, Cassano's capacity to meet the challenge was on full display. The game was on.

Enterprise Architecture

Changing the trajectory of a poor arc is extremely difficult to do. Most leaders and organizations will fail when they try—that is, if they try.

---

44 **Changing the trajectory of a poor decision arc is extremely difficult.**

Inertia within the already cast arc makes it expensive, time-consuming, and energy-draining. Trophy hunters have already taken their positions and are working to capitalize on the arc, perhaps because they have invested in a narrative about where they anticipate it will land, or, in the case of financial arcs, they are short sellers or competitors who gain when another loses. Similarly, inherited teams along the arc have already established their own power hierarchies, modes of communication, routines, and internal odds boards. They have already invested in their projected arc. The blinders are on. Emotions are high. Friction is ever-present. Sometimes circumstances will align where unique, strong, domineering, clever, or charismatic individuals can break the arc and recast it. This is extremely rare. It is the exception rather than the rule. Yet it is where great leaders truly reveal themselves.

45 The larger decision-making enterprise is also coded with a decision archetype.

The immensely more challenging exercise is to build the architecture of the enterprise so that it is more responsive and better able to react to the unique demands placed upon it at any time given the situational context it is most likely to face. Cassano, for example, had little to no ability to react to

46 The decision-making function of an enterprise should be architected to be responsive to the myriad alternative situational contexts it is likely to encounter, not just one.

the changing game in the subprime market. In fact, he worked against change for months, then slow-played FP's reaction thereafter. He had his narrative. His purpose-built machine was humming. His team was small, walled-off, secretive, and singularly focused on doing deals rather than adapting to the unfolding realities of a rapidly changing situational context.[255] Cassano's "fighter" archetype was vulnerable by its very design, as the leader who shapes the enterprise architecture to simply reflect his own decision archetype rather than thrive in new, rapidly changing situational contexts will inevitably face loss. Instead, those who develop an enterprise architecture to intentionally anticipate and interpret the conditions of change will later fare best. They will be in position to capitalize on the change instead of fall victim to it.

There is even more depth to the lesson. Cassano and the FP enterprise violated another of the cardinal rules of Wall Street.

47 The subtle shifts in how the decision arc is progressing will be apparent to some but not all players in the game. Those who can read the shifts possess advantage.

Money is made during periods of change. Cassano had changed FP. It no longer was the nimble player that made money where others could not. It was not responsive to change. The music changed. With the change, he could not make money. Others could. The arc shifted. He did not. Cassano was not culpable. He was simply outplayed. He lacked the judgment and skills to navigate the game imposed upon him. Those who do not hear the music changing are naturally eliminated.

The terrorists attacking Paris sought to exploit the enterprise architecture of the French security forces, hoping to also find a slow-learning and slow-footed foe. They hoped their scattered but coordinated attacks in the darkness of a celebratory Friday night in Paris would reveal a French national security apparatus at its weakest, caught off guard, frightened, emotional, and uncertain of the next move by an opponent lurking in the shadows and threatening to strike again. The attacks could have been the undoing of the French, just as Goldman Sachs's attack on Cassano and FP's small team on its credit derivatives desk was theirs, but with tragically higher losses in the form of thousands of lives lost. The French, however, had architected their national security enterprise to react quickly and effectively in containing the threat in such situations. They had anticipated the need to respond in a changed environment and to do so quickly.

Hundreds were killed or injured over several hours, and the night represents one of France's most tragic in recent history. Even so, it could have been so much worse. Tens of thousands could have been killed or seriously injured if the French security services not had in place effective mechanisms for reacting to a unique threat in a crucible moment. Their enterprise architecture had been designed for this moment. It was responsive and agile, able to make quick judgments, contain the threat, and then eliminate it.

Similarly, across the Atlantic, the White House Situation Room is purposefully architected to react quickly and accurately to new threats and challenges, with operational processes able to purposefully and continuously adapt to the new and unique threats that emerge across the world. Each threat has its own unique arc, each searching for new ways to strike the United States the way viruses adapt to find ways for infecting a host. The host, in turn, has to adapt to the newest incursion quickly. If it cannot, it will die. As such, the White House Situation Room enables the larger US national security apparatus to quickly and effectively change the arc of new hot spots that gurgle up from the goo.

Alignment

It took AIG four CEOs rotating through the turnstile over two years to find alignment between the decision archetype of its leader and the situational context the company faced. In

---

48 There must be alignment between the actor's decision archetype and the situational context in which the decision arc is flowing in order to achieve the highest probability of success.

2009, in the long slog following its bailout, Robert Benmosche took over. AIG was unequivocally the most hated company in America at this point.[256] Executives and employees were leaving, fearful their careers were over if they stayed with the company any longer. Some were being threatened. Liebergall's two little girls left for school in the mornings hidden underneath blankets in the back seat of a car. Their parents told them there were photographers outside trying to take their pictures. The reality was that death threats were being made.[257] The FBI listened in. Security sat outside along the curb. The handful of individuals at AIG who had made mistakes of judgment were long ago fired or had resigned,[258] and the hundreds of thousands of other employees who kept the

AIG ship steady through the storm, continuing to safely house billions in assets around the world, were beaten down.[259] By the time Benmosche entered the game, the trajectory of AIG's stone gliding across the ice was awful. It was a fool's mission. He inherited a company poised for failure.

Something more perverse was going on. AIG had drawn down over $125 billion in taxpayer-backed funds. It would end up drawing down more than $180 billion. This may have been egregious, but it is not the deeper perversity that lies just below the public's consciousness.

Instead, AIG's counterparties on those transactions entered into prior to 2008—which included many large financial institutions that had played similar roles in contributing to the subprime crisis—objected to taking any discount or "haircut" on their exposures.[260] The government was forced to concede. The counterparties were made fully whole, regardless of their sins. The principles of individual culpability or collective responsibility were thrown out the window. The rules of the game shifted once again or perhaps simply returned to the original rules after the brief suspension necessary to navigate the height of the crisis. The banks acted as banks once again. To politicians and the public, it was reprehensible. However, little could be done. The banks had leverage in the game, and the game of global finance favors those who have leverage, right or wrong, culpable or innocent.

All the while, in Washington, DC, politicians continued castigating AIG. Railing against the most hated company in America, which had gone from being one of the most powerful players in the game to the least, was easy. It seemed reasonable. It seemed responsible. It allowed politicians and regulators to set themselves upon a perch of manufactured responsibility, of course ignoring their own years of irresponsibility in allowing the dark markets to grow with little transparency or understanding of the ways in which the red wires and black wires were being woven together.

AIG's day-to-day operations were now under the watchful eye of overseers from the federal government. They were micromanagers. They operated in a heavy-handed manner, dutifully charged with safeguarding the taxpayer funds used to stem the crisis. In fulfilling this mandate, one of their courses of action was to force AIG to liquidate subsidiaries and assets as fast as possible to cover the debts now owed to the Fed. The overseers were forcing a fire sale. Other financial companies were picking at the carcass. To the public and within Washington's political culture, it seemed suitable justice or even revenge for the atrocities of the financial crisis.

The strategy was based upon an even deeper or hidden perversity. It made a weakened AIG only weaker. The weaker AIG became, the less likely it would be able to pay off the taxpayers. The reality was that the bailout monies and the assets bought at fire sale prices would be transferred to the survivors of the crisis, meaning those who had survived the explosives-laden game of musical chairs only to be made whole. The government was forcing a probable outcome that was diametrically opposed to its stated purpose. It pushed AIG's stone away from the bull's-eye, not toward it, and it would benefit most those who had committed similar sins.

Benmosche was a large man with a big voice. Some said he could quickly suck all the oxygen out of a crowded room with his personality.[261] When he took over as AIG's CEO, he saw the perversity being committed by those who had something to gain by shaping the arc in their favor, even if it would forcibly cost taxpayers hundreds of billions and subsidize the gains of others with a measure of blood on their own hands. He became one of the sweepers now charged with trying to redirect the arc of AIG's stone back on course, which was toward full recovery and repayment of all monies owed to taxpayers. Benmosche's message of strength and redemption was motivational for the more than one hundred thousand employees of AIG.[262] The healing could begin. Liebergall said something shifted when Benmosche arrived: "You could feel it."

Benmosche's style of leadership was transformational. It was perfectly aligned to the needs of the moment.[263] However, the message to those who benefited from AIG remaining the most hated company in America, such as the politicians and media, took his message as an afront. Benmosche, consistent with his archetype, wanted to be bold and decisive. The politicians and media wanted him to genuflect before them in submission or subservience. Benmosche could not do it. It was his limitation. The paradox was that if he followed his natural instincts and archetype to bash the politicians and regulators who were forcing a perverse outcome, he risked fueling a further increase in hostilities with political Washington. The gambit, albeit altruistically inspired to Benmosche's way of thinking, would send AIG's puck even farther from the bull's-eye. He would be co-opted into helping Washington sink AIG, regardless of the tremendous loss it would cause American taxpayers.

The situational context of political Washington is very different from Wall Street. The trophies hunted, the language spoken, the devices used to influence public opinion, the platforms possessed to make the case for whatever it deems good or evil in the respective games—are all different. All had the

---

49 Understand the opponent's enterprise archetype and the trophies they hunt.

---

ability to crush AIG's aspirations of regaining health and vitality. Despite what they might otherwise say, the mandarins of political Washington seemed willing to lose hundreds of billions in taxpayer monies if it was necessary to force AIG into bankruptcy, a conclusion to the story reinforcing the narratives that served them well. It was a narrative that could get them reelected and reappointed. Wall Street is a machine. So is political Washington. Benmosche's archetype was wired to succeed at Wall Street. He was horrible in Washington. The error of misalignment once again threatened.

To compensate for the fact that Benmosche's archetype served him very well in one situational context but was a liability in another, AIG did something that would prove prescient. It is a lesson otherwise difficult for many strong-willed leaders to accept. Their decision archetype is an asset in one arena.

---

50 Decision archetypes and their underlying characteristics, both known and unknown to the actor and others, influence or even predetermine their decisions and ultimately their actions.

In a self-reinforcing way, it has fueled their long-running success. It builds confidence. It can also create blindness, intransigence, frustration, and behaviors that directly contribute to defeat when exposed to an alternative situational context, one in which the rules and motivations operate differently, pursuing different trophies, and using different techniques honed to compete and win at a different game. In the case of AIG, the company resolved that Benmosche would stay in his arena, Wall Street. He would lead negotiating a path for getting AIG out of its hole to restore it. Another executive would take point on appeasing the egos and power-seekers in Washington's universe, operating with greater diplomacy and greater recognition for the subtle and not-so-subtle ways of Washington than Benmosche could exhibit. AIG now had two sweepers each respectively focused on keeping AIG's arc in line and on track, working from two different situational contexts, united in their goal of landing AIG on its bull's-eye.

Benmosche stopped the Fed-imposed strategy of selling AIG assets at fire sale prices. He slowed down the process, regrouped, ran better auctions, and secured prices closer to fair value for the assets sold. He sold off more than two dozen businesses. The proceeds were used to pay off $182.3 billion in federal aid, plus another $15.1 billion in profits to US tax-payers. Simultaneously, AIG regained profitability. Washington was kept at bay.

The resurrection of AIG has been described as one of the most successful corporate turnarounds in US history. The stone came to rest on the bull's-eye. Washington became quiet. It had no carcass to stand atop.[264]

Archetype Diversity

One in five American submariners were killed in WWII. It was the deadliest branch of service during the war. For the German enemy, it was far worse. Seven of every ten men in its submarines were killed. It is the warfare of blindness, being blind and killing the blind. It was incredibly lethal.

During WWII, submarine warfare essentially involved diesel-powered boats skimming along the surface and then submerging on electric battery power for relatively short periods of time to surveil, hunt, hide, or evade. Notwithstanding the risk of being killed by enemy assault, the sheer mechanics of submarining made it profoundly dangerous. Many were lost simply due to the failure of the machines. Death would result from fire, asphyxiation, or drowning.

Following the war, submarining only became more dangerous. Nuclear physics moved from the theoretical to the actual. Its arrival had the potential to both advance humanity and hasten its end. The major and minor powers of the world were cast into a race to capture its secrets, seeking to secure any asymmetric advantage as their own.

The Cold War that followed immediately after WWII witnessed the introduction and rise of nuclear-powered submarines. They promised to run nearly silent through the waters and remain submerged for extremely long periods of time.

No longer constrained by their fuel, they could surveil, hunt, hide, or evade for as long as the sheer physical and mental endurance of the men would permit. They were outfitted with nuclear reactors to drive their propulsion systems and could be loaded with nuclear warheads. The risks were immense. An error could be triggered by faulty engineering of the machine or the performance of the men. Either threatened to set off a cataclysmic cascade of humanitarian, political, and ecological tragedies.

The first men to volunteer for service in the new US nuclear navy were unique individuals. They had to be. They were wired differently. They faced lethal risks exponentially greater than their predecessors. The physical, intellectual, and emotional burden of the assignment was immense. One of the greatest challenges in establishing and professionalizing the nuclear navy would be to ensure human performance upon a submarine was its greatest asset, not its greatest liability.

The father of the US nuclear navy was Adm. Hyman Rickover. Unlike the other pioneers of the Nuclear Age, such as Enrico Fermi, J. Robert Oppenheimer, and a host of others, Rickover was not a physicist. Instead, he was a gifted leader of people. He was the overlord of the vast enterprise necessary to design, build, and operate nuclear-powered submarines, encompassing the diverse array of scientific, engineering, supply-chain, organizational, and military-political complexities associated with such a massive and high-risk endeavor. Over the course of a sixty-three-year career, the longest of any navy officer in history and fully encompassing the entirety of the Cold War, Rickover delivered asymmetric advantage for the United States and its allies through a unique leadership approach.

A common error for leaders is to assume, consciously or subconsciously, that there is a prototype decision archetype for any enterprise. The wisdom is that there is one ideal. Rickover, however, understood that a vast array of differing decision archetypes within the emerging nuclear navy must be embraced to gain the highest levels of human performance across the larger enterprise. Applying a prototypical decision archetype to the enterprise would lead to underperformance or even failure.

Each archetype must instead be aligned with the unique problem or mission before people in a distinct command. It

---

51 Enterprises facing complex situational contexts are strengthened by empowering a diverse array of decision archetypes within their organization, each best aligned to solving the various unique problems the enterprise will encounter.

---

must align to the situational context of that command's areas of responsibility. For example, to achieve the monumental engineering feat of constructing an entirely new class of submarines, the nuclear navy had to attract the best creative minds and the best engineers. It needed innovators and out-of-the-box thinkers, not rule followers, conformists, or traditional military men. Creatives and engineers focused on innovative or break-the-mold thinking would not perform at their best in the traditional command-and-control governance style of the military.

Despite being very much a military man himself whose personal archetype favored structure and authority, Rickover understood that his archetype was but one crayon in the box. He needed representation of all the colors. Consequently, he not only allowed but embraced his engineers' differences. They could dress as civilians even if they were military personnel. They could have long hair. They could adapt their schedules. They could be quirky. All as long as they performed brilliantly against their specific mandate. The traditional hierarchies and power structures of a military organization were allowed to recede. Consequently, in its place, a meritocracy emerged that rewarded intelligence, innovative thinking, creative problem-solving, and accomplishment over rank, power, or strength of personality.

Hank Greenberg did something similar when he set up FP in Connecticut. He was chief of the AIG tribe. He had his own pronounced decision archetype.[265] He was at the top of the pyramidical hierarchy. He was tough on his reports. He was a micromanager. He constantly scrutinized employees' exercise of judgment, rewarding those who excelled and castigating or dismissing those who made errors. He led as he had in WWII and the Korean War, as though life were combat. As a result, AIG became a machine.

Yet the FP subsidiary was allowed to operate differently. It operated more like a think tank. The organization rewarded creative thinking. Intellect was more valuable than machismo. Hank knew that the creatives needed to work differently and think differently, and would find success along decidedly different arcs than those AIG teams that stewarded over the more regulated, more traditionally structured insurance subsidiaries.

In both cases, the enterprise architecture of the organization was carefully designed to align with the decision arcs the teams would encounter, including through the diverse situational context in which these enterprises worked. Diverse decision archetypes were embraced within these enterprises rather than tamped down or smothered. As a result, Rickover fathered a nuclear navy that came to possess an asymmetric advantage over the Soviets for decades, and the first decade of FP's existence was one of the most successful ventures in Wall Street history.

Long Arcs

Enterprises must prepare their organizations for the long arcs upon which judgment will be exercised in a myriad of daily decisions. Doing so builds strength and stability for the

---

52 Long arcs track against large-scale systemic shifts in the situational context.

---

enterprise. The failure to prepare well for those decisions that travel long arcs will result in intense, poorly anticipated crisis conditions, a situational context in which judgment can be impaired by a lack of curation and the convergence of numerous adverse indicators.

As WWII drew to a close, the world faced an uncertain future. New long arcs that shaped the global balance of power and the fragility of peace were unfolding. The geopolitical and economic axes of the world were shifting. The seeds of the coming Cold War were planted, and at the same time, the mysteries of the Nuclear Age were being revealed. Rickover's career nestled at the intersection point of these shifts, each influencing the path of future decision arcs. Everything ahead was new. The opponents would be many.

Yet the opportunity was significant. Rickover was charged with launching into the great unknown before him to build the nuclear navy. It was a somewhat similar challenge the Wall Street quants would face when approaching Hank in the late 1980s. They saw tremendous shifts in the financial markets. New arcs were being created. They could see their beginnings. Others could not. There would be legions of problems before them that would be deemed too hard for others to solve. If they could unravel these unfolding problems unsolvable to others, the opportunity for AIG would be significant. For both the naval commander and the financial quants, there was no predetermined playbook for launching into the unknown. Instead, their success or failure would be determined by their continuous exercise of judgment at each of the inflection points that would no doubt arise along the new long arcs of decision-making before them.

Several lessons emerge from their experiences. First, both Rickover and his early corps, as well as Hank and the quants, understood their launch point to the long arc before

---

53 Identify the launch point whereby you inherit an unfolding decision arc.

---

them. Each arc in its own unique way pointed to vast oceans of unknown before them. The challenges would be immensely complex. The domains of knowledge required to discover a path forward would be underdeveloped. New disciplines, mental models, and experimentation would be required. Mistakes would have to be made. New bodies of knowledge would have to be curated by different kinds of thinkers arranged into new kinds of organizational structures.

It would have been easy for Rickover or Hank to simply

apply the organizational models and governance structures that pervaded their already massive organizations, including, respectively, the US Navy and AIG. Those models had already proven successful. It would be easy to naturally extend them to their new enterprises. Familiarity is easier to sell than novelty.

Rickover and Hank, however, had to do things differently. Their challenges were too unique. The waters ahead were too uncertain. New organizational structures designed to drive their respective enterprises toward entirely new decisions that lie ahead had to be built. They needed to be able to unwind complex problems and reward creativity, innovation, and out-of-the box thinking. Traditional structures designed to meet other kinds of problems would fail. Rickover and Hank both knew where their launch points were for what would be the long learning curves necessary to succeed in their respective new domains, which in both cases was very early. They intentionally architected their respective enterprises to do problem-solving for the long decision arcs unfolding before them.

In contrast to the choices made by Rickover and Hank, Alan Greenspan and his peer regulators failed this test when they had the chance.[266] More specifically, they, too, had a launch point pinned early onto the learning curve necessary to navigate the great ocean of unknown before them—in this case, the dark markets of unregulated derivatives and other financial innovations that grew exponentially through the

---

54 Past patterns, values, cognitive structures, organizational inertia, and other factors lead to players possessing blind spots that hinder their ability to manage a decision arc.

1990s and early 2000s. Instead of wading into the great unknown to discover the best path through, however, they deferred. They closed their eyes instead of opening them. They argued that a "regulatory chill" would occur if they waded into the unfolding market to understand its emergence from the primordial goo of the financial markets. They thought that if they took a peek down the path, creativity would be hindered. The quants and financial engineers would sit on their hands. Capital would not free up, and more productive economic purposes would not be financed. However, because they did not wade in to the dark waters before them, eyes wide open, the great ocean nearly swallowed their successors and the global economy a short few years later.

There is further dimension to this learning. The process of wading in, working up the learning curve, being willing to give space to the creative thinkers, allowing mistakes to be made, and organizing the processes and the people who will influence the shape of the decisions and how judgment will be exercised is not a random one. It is an intentionally

---

55 Great decisions in crucible moments have been intentionally curated.

---

curated process. Hank stayed close enough to FP to know what the quants were up to and threatened to come after them "with pitchforks" if they did anything that jeopardized AIG's AAA rating. Rickover was intimately immersed in the functioning of his organization, understanding the mistakes, becoming privy to the new learnings, rooting down into how his officers and engineers were thinking about problems, and finding their incremental successes as well as experiencing points of stagnation and failure, then endlessly iterating upon these learnings to build a formidable organization and weapon of asymmetric advantage in the Cold War.

At their respective launch points, Rickover and Hank were eager students upon whom initiation began at an introductory level, progressed through more advanced levels, then went even further to refine their expertise so that they exceeded all others in their respective domains. Their judgment improved as they encountered new decision arcs, leveraging new enterprise archetypes. In turn, they encouraged a diverse set of thinkers with their own unique decision archetypes and installed governance models that curated rather than suffocated the growth that would be required going forward.

In contrast, Greenspan and his peer regulators knew something phenomenal was unfolding before them. Yet, faced with the same launch point to a daunting learning curve that lurked before them, they advocated not walking the path. Their choice was intentional. As a result, their successors in 2006 and 2007 were forced to cram in order to learn what harms lurked, quickly trying to dig into the dark markets and learn what they did not know, trying to understand the risks, and attempting to get their arms around the size and nature of the problem to fashion a response. As the five days in September 2008 under Geithner's leadership shows, in the end, the decision-making in a crucible moment was an exercise in experimentation, with the parties playing a game of chicken to see who would bear the burden. Decisions were forced by crisis, not the careful curation of a long arc.

In hindsight, now knowing how close the world came to a full-scale economic meltdown that September, to have not waded into a new market unfolding in order to better understand it, let alone possibly steward its more thoughtful growth, was not just an error or oversight. It was reckless. Those charged with protecting the markets had instead elected to turn away.[267] As a result, they were not privy to the mistakes in judgment being made by countless others pursuing their own decision arcs to exploit what they perceived as vast new oceans of opportunity in the dark waters before them. The Financial Crisis Inquiry Commission concluded, "The crisis was the result of human action and inaction, not of Mother Nature or computer models gone haywire."[268] In the end, the successor regulators and market participants were caught off guard. The crisis was not a surprise. It was inevitable. Those charged with stewarding the path forward had failed to understand the long arcs unfolding before them.[269]

Evolution

W hen Rickover began building the nuclear navy, the officers in the inaugural generation were considered cowboys. Every moment of their career was on the knife's edge, teetering between life and death. These were tough and brash men. Many were not great managers. They were renegades, the kind of people who gravitated to danger. Rickover knew he needed to groom these cowboys into a professional corps of commanders, executive officers, and senior enlisted personnel. They would have to come together as a unified body and adhere to well-practiced processes for acquiring information and making decisions. Shepherding the evolution of this first generation of leaders was among his top priorities.

Rickover's engineering of human performance formed the very foundation of the nuclear navy. He personally interviewed every young officer seeking to join the nuclear branch, including the young Ensign T. W. "Ted" Hack, newly graduated from Villanova University. Rickover required extensive reporting by all officers in written form. These infamous "Rickover Reports" enabled him to keep a close pulse on progress, but perhaps even more importantly, to understand how the authors thought through problems. He reportedly went so far as to have secretaries retrieve from the wastebaskets the mimeographs of prior drafts of reports by his underlings in order to see how their thinking evolved, where reports might be burnished to cover up failings or underperformance, and to understand what these personnel continued to find unsolvable.

By the time Hack took command of the USS *Guardfish* in the mid-1980s, the era of the rough and abrasive cowboy commander had sunset. The US Navy was now on to its next

---

56 Decision archetypes within the enterprise should continuously evolve to meet ever-higher standards for judgment well exercised.

---

generation of officers. The command had evolved to achieve higher levels of human performance. Commanding officers were chief executive officers well trained in not only the engineering and operation of their nuclear boats but even greater managers of tight-knit communities of men who lived and worked together for months on end in a steel tube without windows, being the hunter, being the prey, and facing their own mortality with each moment.

Rickover also understood that any asymmetric advantage would only partly be based upon the engineering of its nuclear submarines. The balance of success would significantly depend upon optimizing the process by which thousands of individuals could effectively perceive the unique challenges and dream of the ways to pierce through these otherwise extraordinary

---

57 Asymmetric advantage is gained by a player through careful curation of the decision-making process.

---

barriers before them. His gift was to unlock the cognitive, emotional, and behavioral intelligence of those in his command, wherever those capabilities may reside, and then continuously raise the caliber of leadership. He focused on enabling his team to push into their blind spots to discover the depths of what was not known, reaching into their fears and beyond their egos to mine the potential and mitigate the risks. Rickover's methods harnessed the extraordinary capacities of his diverse people. He knit them together to create his most powerful asset. He evolved the management capacities of the nuclear navy, maturing and modernizing the modes of leadership, governance, and communications so that it became a critical differentiator upon which asymmetric advantage could be achieved in the domain of Cold War submarine warfare.

Short Arcs

Some decision arcs travel a very short span. Decisions will need to be made quickly, under pressure, and without prolonged study or analysis. To prepare for short arcs, for exam-

---

58 When a decision is required quickly or is forced by external events, the probability of success is dependent upon prior preparation, including preconditioning the decision-making processes and prior training of the team.

---

ple, the command and crew of a submarine drill endlessly for a series of anticipated crucible moments that can arise quickly, either opportunistically or defensively. Whether patrolling for other submarines and ships, dropping special forces close to targets, engaging in evasive maneuvers when detected, or positioning for ballistic action, there are any number of potential launch points to the decision that will need to be made.

From these launch points, the command will quickly work through a prescribed analytical model and decision tree that has been developed and iterated upon in order to minimize the types of cognitive errors that occur under moments of uncertainty and stress. The decision arcs become routinized to the greatest extent possible in order to minimize the risks of judgment poorly executed within the unfolding crucible. The objective is to create highly responsive teams that have developed the muscle memory and autonomous flows to minimize errors as well as reduce the cognitive load to process their actions so that it can be reserved to process new information, changes, and deviations from the anticipated norm.

Similarly, the White House Situation Room is purposely designed to manage short decision arcs. More specifically, when a hot spot flares, its purpose is to determine where the launch point is for that unique decision arc arising. The potential span of an emerging arc is a critical first component of the analysis.

For Obama and his response to the unfolding Paris attacks, based upon the gathering of facts by the national security agencies spread across the US government, convened and distilled by the White House Situation Room, the distance between the launch point and a decision ultimately was determined to be somewhere between fourteen and eighteen hours. The White House Situation Room would monitor this assessment carefully to determine if certain events lengthened or compressed this span, such as if the terrorists attacked or threatened to attack a US target imminently.

For President Hollande, in contrast, the distance between the launch point of his new decision arc, that being the first explosion at the soccer stadium, and his exercise of judgment to best protect the French people could be as short as several minutes, perhaps even less.

The decision arcs inherited by Hollande and Obama respectively from the same launch point on that fateful Paris night were in fact immensely different. Accordingly, this changed everything about the appropriate governance models each would deploy, the language they would respectively use, and the points at which they individually would be forced to make decisions. Hollande had minutes to exercise judgment.

59 The behavior of the decision arc is significantly dependent upon its anticipated duration.

Obama had a night. Hollande went on the attack. Obama went to sleep—deferring the exercise of his judgment until consulting with his National Security Council the following morning and before boarding Air Force One bound for Europe.

The playbook of the White House Situation Room is expressly constructed so as to determine the span of the decision arc and then react accordingly. From this initial assessment, the greater US national security enterprise can then curate the decision and the variables affecting judgment so that it may be appropriately exercised. Determining the launch point for a decision arc, relative to the time span and nature of the decision required of the moment, requires developing well-curated processes, discipline, and acumen.

Revealing Decision Outcomes

In Syria, a truck driver tends the fire below his kettle. There is not much else to do but drink tea and smoke cigarettes. He has been waiting, as he always does, sometimes for days on end.

The oil field is just down the road from Abu Kamal, a town settled on the edge of the Euphrates River along Syria's border with Iraq. It has been a way station for traders shuttling among the tribes of people for millennia. In this morning light, several hundred other drivers with tired eyes and tar-stained hands move about slowly in their own morning routines. They are the silent ones who travel through and across the desert, making enough at the periphery of the most present and long-festering war to feed their own families back home, wherever that might be.

The truck driver will buy oil from those who now control the fields just beyond. It used to be the Syrian government. It is now ISIS. He does not care about their cause, quite frankly. He suspects most of the ones he deals with don't care, either. They just need something to belong to, be a part of, and survive another day. Everyone has their reality to muster through. He has his. They have theirs. He needs to get only enough oil to fill his truck, safely navigate the border when traveling back to Iraq, and make a bit of profit. Perhaps he will get a load today. Perhaps it will be tomorrow.

ISIS has taken control of more than 80 percent of Syria's oil fields.[270] They now own a virtual monopoly. They have become the privileged, the powerful who determine the rules, control the flow, and harvest the profit. It is one of the cardinal rules. They make more than $1 million each day selling oil to truckers like the several hundred lined up just outside Abu Kamal. More than half of ISIS's $800 million in revenue per year comes from this black market.[271]

It is a tyrannical ideology built upon a criminal economy in a desert where the order is determined by the most powerful or the most brutal, where the assets are stolen, and where the rules always benefit the taker. It is an economic enterprise that enables ISIS to control vast swaths of land, trade for guns and military equipment, and maintain the extensive supply chain necessary to feed its followers and their families. Year after year, the ISIS economic enterprise grows more sophisticated, maturing beyond the petty crimes of a ragtag band of radicals and disaffected youth searching for something through which they can gain a sense of purpose and belonging, ambling about the deserts of Iraq and Syria in the brutish comradery that rises from the shocking psychological traumas rendered by war and savagery.

ISIS is now evolving and adapting to the new realities it faces. It is becoming a sophisticated organization with pervasive networks able to profit from all economic activity within its areas of controlled lands. In its own way, it is building its own beautiful machine.

ISIS has grown at such a pace and level of sophistication that it is at last able to take its aspirations global. It will take its fight into the heart of those nations flying fighters and gunships above it. It will train, finance, and deploy cells of agents into Europe and America. It will kill and disrupt the very supply chains of its enemies, just as they try to disrupt

ISIS's supply chains of money, oil, and weaponry. It will seek to wound them where they are most vulnerable. It will seek to level catastrophic damages on an enemy abroad, and it will use asymmetric warfare to do so. Its newly acquired oil profits will make it so.

The Iraqi driver pokes again at the fire below the kettle with a stick. He hears the whispering sound of a jet approach just a few seconds before it is above him. He sees other drivers run out into the desert. Some seek shelter in the ratty tents they have set up in the scrub along the road. He stands still and looks up. In the last fourteen years of war all around him, he has become well versed in the aircraft and the flags of the nations that fly them. It is an A-10 Thunderbolt II attack plane. The Americans call it the Warthog. He watches to see if it will drop a bomb near the refinery or spin up its guns on those scampering below. It does not.

It is getting harder for the drivers to buy oil from ISIS. Those now waiting along the road to Abu Kamal have long ago grown used to seeing jets streak across the skies. Very often, those jets will target a refinery or some other part of the oil infrastructure. It usually takes the oil engineers only a day or two to get the flow back up and running after a strike. Over the past month, it has taken longer. The strikes are coming closer to the heart of the infrastructure.[272] There is nothing the drivers can do about any of it except sit along the side of the road, drink tea, smoke cigarettes, and wait.

Something is different about this jet's path. It flies low over the column of trucks leading to the refinery. Once past the refinery, the pilot pulls the nose of the plane up steeply. The plane banks to the right. The driver spots three other A-10s loitering about. Two American AC-130 Spectre gunships circle a bit higher.[273] The driver then sees something unusual. It is a leaflet wafting down from the sky. It lands near his kettle. He walks over and picks it up. It says in Arabic: *Get out of your trucks now, and run away from them. Warning: airstrikes are coming. Oil trucks will be destroyed. Get away from your oil trucks immediately. Do not risk your life.*[274]

In the theater of war, lots of things are said. The only thing that matters, however, is what is done. The driver suspects the leaflets could be a ploy, designed to simply scare enough of the drivers away to slow the money coming into the coffers of ISIS. It might work. It might slow things down for a day or two, but the drivers will be back. They have to come back. They need the oil. They need to trade.[275] They need the money for their own lives scratched out of living in a desert, among never-ending wars, with the locals paying the price for whatever ideology their ever-changing occupier espouses.

What the driver does not know is that there were a series of attacks on Friday night in Paris. What the driver could not know is that yesterday morning, Obama met with his national security team before boarding Air Force One to attend a G20 summit in Türkiye .[276] What the driver would not know is that Obama had several choices before him yesterday. He chose one in the quiet sanctum of the White House Situation Room.

Obama has given the go-ahead on Saturday morning to a strategy that pushes the trajectory of his decision arc up a handful of degrees. It now falls somewhere between moderation and brazen retribution for the Paris attacks. Forty minutes after the driver reads the leaflet, the US attack planes and gunships strafe the column of trucks that bring money to ISIS in exchange for their stolen oil. One hundred sixteen civilian tanker trucks are destroyed. No civilians are killed.[277]

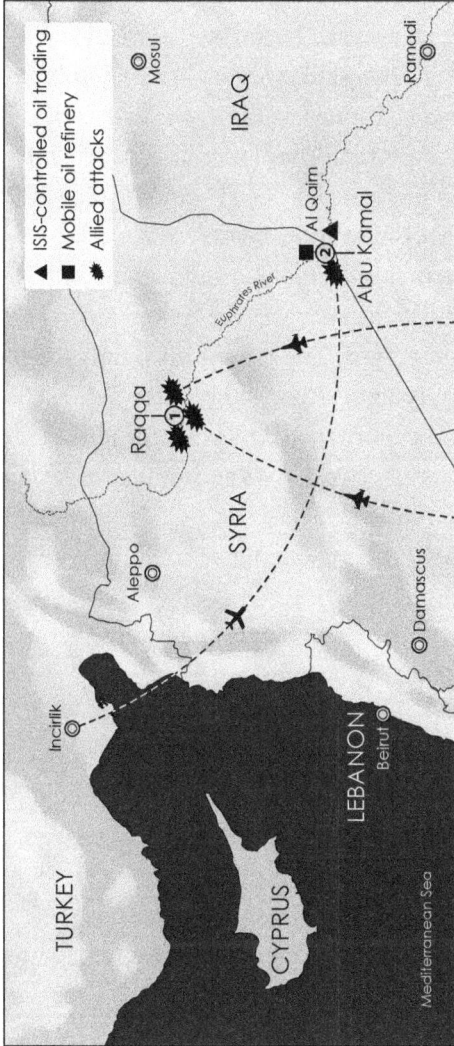

RETALIATORY ATTACKS – SUNDAY, NOVEMBER 15, 2015

TURKEY
Incirlik
CYPRUS
LEBANON
Beirut
Mediterranean Sea
SYRIA
Aleppo
Raqqa
Damascus
Euphrates River
Al Qaim
Abu Kamal
IRAQ
Mosul
Ramadi

Legend:
▲ ISIS-controlled oil trading
■ Mobile oil refinery
✹ Allied attacks

① After coordination with the United States, including receiving pre-designated strike packages, France sends 12 planes from Jordan and the UAE, including 10 fighters, to drop 20 bombs on ISIS targets around its de facto capital of Raqqa.

② In an escalation of the American-led campaign against ISIS-controlled infrastructure in Syria, the United States sends A-10s and AC-130 aircraft in an airstrike which targets and destroys 116 civilian oil tankers waiting to be loaded with ISIS-controlled oil.

The strikes are the first time Obama has authorized the military to take out civilian components of the ISIS black market supply chain. It is a shift of sorts in the Obama doctrine and a statement of America's reaction to the Paris attacks. It is the sort of shift, however, that most Americans will never come to know about. It will likely be only a blip in their news of yet another strike in a desert far away, little noticed and most likely soon forgotten. The hoped-for insight into what could prove to be a momentous decision on the long arc of the Global War on Terror may never be fully revealed.

The driver's truck is a smoking hull. Along with all the other drivers that day, he survives the American attacks, but his livelihood is destroyed. The fate of his family is now uncertain. Obama fully understands the potential of such aggression to radicalize more men and women and lead them to join the criminal enterprises of ISIS and similar organizations that lurk in the darker corners of the world. The calculus of his momentous decision is changing a little bit in the wake of the Paris attacks—but not a lot.

Over the course of the next forty-eight hours, the larger dimensions of Obama's decisions on a fateful Saturday morning become evident. In addition to the attack on the convoy, the US military has provided the French preplanned strike packages.[278] On this Sunday at 7:50 p.m. CET, French fighters launch Operation Chammal.[279] They target leadership, logistics, and recruiting locations in and around Raqqa, the Syrian city that is the headquarters for ISIS.[280]

In Europe, American intelligence will support French and Belgian intelligence in identifying and searching for suspects associated with the Paris bombings.

On Monday, September 16, in the wake of the G20 summit, Obama and other world leaders will presumably have some success in their conversations with Putin, as evidenced by Putin's agreement to launch parallel strikes against ISIS targets in Syria.[281]

What Obama does not do is put US troops on the ground in Syria. His political opponents back in Washington, DC, clamor to do more against ISIS. They ratchet up their rhetorical pressure on Obama.

Obama is moving the decision arc, but subtly. He emerges the morning after the Paris attacks resolved to do a bit more, be a bit more aggressive, to support the French as they intensify their aggression. However, he reveals that despite the pressure to do more, he is willing to turn the heat up only a couple of degrees.

---

60 Trigger points along the decision arc reveal the inner calculus of the decision maker, including their susceptibility to influence or pressure, as well as the flexibility of their values and decision architecture.

Obama's response tells us about the moment. Perhaps more importantly, his patterns and reactions reveal to us the coding that may foretell how he will respond to the next national security crisis.

Republicans will watch. Democrats will watch. The international community will watch. ISIS will watch. They search for clues as to where the arc will traverse next.

The Mark

By hunting the trigger points within an unfolding decision arc, revealing the hardwired codes that underpin decision archetypes and understanding its complex dynamics, a player in the game can place a mark.

The mark is an intentionally placed attack point along the arc. It is the point at which a player seeks to cause the arc to

---

61 Place a mark or be the mark.

---

inflect, bend, or even end. The mark is significant. If placed well, it can create the path to victory. If misplaced, it can impair the player or perhaps eliminate them from the game.

If a player is the unwitting target of a mark placed (which they often and ideally are), and they fail to act or react effectively, they will lose.

In 1985, for example, after months of study, deliberation, and preparation, the US Navy placed its mark on the Akula. The Soviets lost. The Americans won.

In 2003, Attorney General Eliot Spitzer put a mark on Hank Greenberg when the opportunity presented itself. Hank was forced out of the company he had built. Spitzer won.

In 2007, Goldman Sachs had billions of dollars at risk in the subprime credit market.[282] It found the point where it sought to inflect the arc moving forward. It placed an unprecedented capital call on AIG; the mark was placed. Two years later, the results were clear.[283] Goldman Sachs won.

In 2015, ISIS terrorists marked Paris on a Friday evening.[284] Within twenty-four hours and for months on end thereafter, ISIS was pounded with tremendous retributory attacks by those countries allied in the Global War on Terror, including the United States, France, and Russia, at least for a while. ISIS, in this instance, misplaced its mark. Its enemies had superior methods for curating decisions and their actions. The pendulum of asymmetric advantage swung quickly from favoring the terrorists in their surprise but sophisticated attacks to the American and European powers. The terrorists misplaced their mark. As a result, this group was neutered. The coalition won.

The mark reveals a tremendous amount about the game and how judgment is exercised.

Common Errors

There are numerous ways in which judgment can be poorly exercised when forced by the pressures of a crucible moment.

New learning curves emerge quickly.

Decision-making processes become corrupted.

Personalities overcome logic.

Perceptions take on filters.

---

62 Judgment is adversely affected by common and avoidable errors.

Sensitivities distort.

Emotions create higher highs and lower lows.

Through this darkened briar littered with challenges, uncertainties, and fears, a range of common errors can be averted simply through acute awareness of what they look like and where they lurk.

Ego over Mission

"It is never about you," Maren Brooks said of the White House Situation Room. "It is about the mission."

The White House Situation Room is a den of ego. With any given national security incident, this office becomes the cen-

---

63 Decisions should be made in service to the mission rather than the decision maker's ego.

---

tral node through which the most senior executive officers of the United States—including the President, Vice President, National Security Advisory, Secretary of Defense, Secretary of State, Central Intelligence Agency, National Security Agency, and the heads of another dozen agencies, each possibly with an additional senior advisor or two—convene. To the person, they are all extremely intelligent, extremely accomplished, highly confident, politically astute, and career-striving individuals.

The same is true of the cohort of bank executives convened by Geithner on that fateful Friday evening in New York in 2008. Each would have extremely strong egos. It is who they are. It is where their success begins.

It can also be their downfall.

There is virtue in a strong ego. It protects the individual and drives their motivation. It is the *I* in their subconsciousness and reveals itself to us in their decisions and actions. It drives their worldview and values. Their first question to each challenge or opportunity is, "How does this affect me?" Then and only then do they begin to solve the problem before them. A healthy ego is required of leaders who face decision-making in critical moments. It is the source of their strength and confidence. It grounds them. It protects them.

An unhealthy ego biases the observation and analysis in favor of the decision-maker's own self-interest over the mission. Poor choices ensue. It can become very dangerous.

Being in service to the mission requires giving primacy to the collective interest in the choices to be made. The *I* is subverted. *We* becomes paramount. The greatest leaders are those who serve a cause greater than themselves. Some go even beyond this, working in service to thousands or millions of people they don't know. They work on behalf of innocents, children, soldiers, shareholders, taxpayers, the nation, or those others who need their protection, their advocacy, and their care, but are unknown, faceless, or defenseless. These are the leaders who become remembered in history for their benevolence and valor. The public craves them.

Intransigent Narratives

Gene Park warned Cassano of tremendous risks within the subprime mortgage market. He did so three years before the peak of the 2008 financial crisis.[285]

About a year later after Park's warning, Cassano began a strategy of cautiously reducing FP's exposures.[286] A year after that, Goldman Sachs placed the first-ever capital call on FP. Eight months later, Cassano was asked to retire.[287] The time span between Park shooting off the first warning flare and Cassano's forced resignation was about two and a half years.

If the story of the financial crisis is merely about the five days in September 2008 in which the markets spiraled uncontrollably toward cataclysm, then the story is incomplete. It would be easy to miss the legion of errors made by sophisticated regulators and financial institutions of all stripes for more than a decade leading up to those five climactic days. The story is one of both long arcs and short ones. Errors were made by many along both trajectories.

Cassano made several. The factual foundation of his narrative, as he understood it, was not necessarily wrong. Cassano maintained throughout the long arc that FP's risk exposure was infinitesimally small when viewed amid the vast ocean of risk coursing through the global financial markets. Generally speaking, this was correct.[288] He was right.[289]

Cassano's error was in the way he locked in on his narrative with such fervor, it created a blind spot. He was reluc-

64 Blinding commitment to a personal narrative can be a weakness.

tant to understand, or perhaps simply to admit, that the larger situational context was shifting slowly along the long arc.[290] While his interpretation may have been technically correct, the situational context in which his view was conceived was changing. He could not—or would not—see it.

Cassano was not adapting fast enough to the realities of each passing moment. More specifically, Cassano kept his eye focused on the rate of default by homeowners, student loan borrowers, credit card holders, and others that might create credit default risk in the underlying instruments FP was backing. His perceptual scope was too narrow.

Other risks were coming to the forefront. FP's structural hedge seemed tight.[291] However, FP had allowed a change to their agreements that created a new portal for risk to enter. A new provision allowed a counterparty to place a collateral call on FP if AIG's ratings were downgraded. When Gold-

65 Unfolding dynamics along the decision arc will reveal the disparities among the players in their ability to perceive, decode, and act or react to the unfolding changes.

man Sachs exercised its right under the call provision, Cassano was caught flat-footed. Then, because these were dark markets that could easily move on the rumors and emotion that course through the endless chatter among the market participants, if one counterparty places a collateral call, it can spook others into doing the same. As collateral calls come in, a trickle at first but threatening to become a torrent, an institution like FP being targeted can run short on cash, unable to move those assets they can quickly liquidate or access their short-term borrowing facilities that purr under normal market conditions. This is liquidity risk.

As the torrent grows, a second risk manifests. When the number of financial institutions being targeted by collateral calls increases—each growing weaker as they deplete cash, liquid assets, and short-term borrowings, all being knit together with the red wires and black wires that inextricably link several dozen global financial institutions together—any single failure in the network risks triggering a cascade of failures taking them all down. This is systemic risk.

These two latter risks were not modeled by FP's retained academics.

They were not accounted for in the structural hedge.

They were not contemplated in Cassano's narrative. He was locked in.

Locking in on a narrative makes the decision maker immobile. They trod through the landscape before them wearing concrete boots, unable to react with more agility. They cling to the nuggets of information that support their positions and shunt off others, seeking to rationalize positions. They listen to those they feel are playing on the same team and push away those who are not, disregarding alternative viewpoints. They can become dismissive or even combative when there is dissent.

The vulnerability can sneak up on the decision maker.

66 When a new or unanticipated decision arc emerges, a new learning curve is immediately presented. Those players able to master the learning curve the quickest and most astutely will emerge the strongest.

Agitated environments create new pressures.

The situational context shifts quickly.

New assessments have to be done to understand what is happening,

The learning curve has to cycle very quickly, oftentimes too quickly for the decision maker and their teams to climb it with speed and acumen.

The noise is significant, with lots of clamor, wild opinions, drama, and speculation.

There is friction and conflict.

Bosses demand answers from managers. At AIG, headquarters started asking lots of questions of FP. Counterparties started asking tough questions in order to understand their own risks. Auditors started thinking about how to cover their asses. Ratings agencies changed from willing enablers to skittish critics. Those regulators who had sat on their hands for years now started to circle.

The media and industry commentators fed on the drama, fanning the flames. Short sellers began locking in on their prey. Law firms representing shareholders started sharpening their blades.

The pressures forced a decision maker like Cassano to dig into a position and defend it, word for word, again and again, never giving an inch. The defender believes if they give one inch in the narrative, it will be perceived as a sign of weakness or vulnerability. Opponents and competitors love it. The self-reinforcing nature of an intransigent narrative completes itself.

The prey weakens itself.

Advocacy before Facts

In the wake of the disastrous 1961 Bay of Pigs invasion of Cuba, President John F. Kennedy determined that the methods and processes for making US national security decisions was deeply flawed. The intelligence he was provided lacked integrity. The facts were not the facts. They were interpretations colored by the biases of the individuals and myriad institutions that knit together to create the national security apparatus. As a result, Kennedy's decision-making suffered. He survived the crisis but emerged battered and bruised.

To remedy the failings, Kennedy created the White House Situation Room. Its mandate was simple. Its sole purpose was to render the most accurate set of facts about the bubbling hot spots around the world that could rapidly implicate the United States and force the president into a position where a critical decision must be made quickly. Stated another way, the mandate of the White House Situation Room was to mitigate the influence of self-serving bureaucratic fiefdoms, power politics, and the flaws of personal assumptions and biases of those who touched the process on its path toward a presidential decision.

The logic of a mandate to gather the facts, and only the facts, is simple to understand. To implement it, however, is immensely challenging.

As hot spots around the world gurgle and seethe, increasing in intensity, then receding or even vanishing, potentially reappearing elsewhere with even more intensity or subtlety, the apparent facts are often cryptic, conflicting, and confusing. They are colored by those who gather them, those who transmit them, and those who interpret them.

67 Gather the facts before interpretation or action.

In the run-up to any momentous decision, whether it be a national security incident, navigating the waters of a choppy subprime credit market, or imagining what lies somewhere beyond the steel hull of a windowless submarine reliant only on the interpretations of acoustic hums and murmurs heard by a sonarman, establishing the facts with accuracy and reliability is of paramount importance and immense challenge.

Misinterpretations, false readings, intentional manipulation, decoys, deception, and incompetence can lead to catastrophic outcomes, whether possibly triggering a nuclear war in the Caribbean (as during the Bay of Pigs) or the Sea of Japan (as when hunting the Akula), sending the global economy into a death spiral or sparking a conflagration after terrorist-driven attacks in Europe.

Any of these distinct situations reflects the common paradox of no participant in the game ever possessing a full or accurate picture of the game; instead, each acts like the blind men in the fable who describe an elephant, compounded by a child's game of telephone.[292] By the time the message reaches its end point, it bears little relationship to the message at the start. Each actor in the chain hears those pieces of the story that stand out to them and that they believe are most important, inevitably sloughing off pieces or distorting remainders.

It can get worse. Short timelines and unstable triggers in the minefield of an emerging fact pattern viewed by different blind men watching the tension adds intensity and sensitivity to the one's perception of the situation. Their different worldviews, values, belief systems, and experiences only amplify the confusion. The smallest shift can dramatically reset the

---

68 **The deeper dynamics within an unfolding decision arc will be confusing to teams facing challenges. There will be an increase in friction, emotion, and bad behaviors, which will affect their ability to effectively respond to or capitalize on new opportunities created.**

---

course of history, the legacy of leaders, and the lives of millions. The elephant is no longer an elephant. The Paris terrorists are impossible to define. The subprime credit market is no longer what it once was. The Soviet Navy recedes back into the stealthy dark.

Returning to one of the core codes of decision-making in crucible moments, the White House Situation Room's mandate is simply to establish the "what" of a situation, not the "why" or "What comes next?"

The White House Situation Room is charged with pulling a picture from the dark fog somewhere out there and drawing it in closer and closer until it becomes more in focus, the shades of gray shifting into lines of black and white, and only then allowing color to resolve into the image.

This function is also its limit. The White House Situation Room does not try to explain what the facts mean. Instead, analysis and interpretation of the facts is the mandate deeded separately to the NSC. The NSC then works in consultation with the State Department, the CIA, the NSA, the Department of Defense, the Department of Homeland Security, and myriad additional agencies to give meaning to the fact patterns, color them, determine alternative courses of action, set probabilities for each, and make recommendations to the president as to the preferred path forward. The president retains ultimate responsibility for making the decision to act or to hold, to increase the intensity or moderate it, to zig or to zag.

The decision arc is never perfect, but it is highly curated; it is the president's judgment that ultimately determines the course of action.

Kennedy set a precedent in 1961 for how national security decisions are made. It is a precedent that has been inherited by each successive president since then. Some have accepted its wisdom readily; others have let the lines between fact-gathering and interpretation blur once again, only to pay the price.[293]

The lineage adapts and improves over time. The heirs to the lineage learn from mistakes. They study the after-action

---

69 To increase probabilities of success, continuously iterate upon the processes and methods for understanding the unfolding decision arc, as well as how judgment will be exercised by the players at key inflection points.

---

reports of each crisis to achieve new learnings, integrating them into the operational policies for how to handle the next crisis lurking in the dark.

On a Friday afternoon more than four decades after Kennedy established this precedent, Obama set to work to gather and validate the facts emerging from Paris. A day later, he and the NSC evaluated the fact pattern, provided their interpretations of the causes and implications of the terrorist attacks, and set probabilities for what would or should come next.

Decisions were made. Judgment was exercised.

The French were aided. Raids in France quickly ensued. Bombs were dropped in Syria. The tail stemming from the arc of the attacks was shortened.

Fallacy of Success

F P's financial performance under Cassano was astounding. Revenue soared in 2004 and again in 2005. Deal volume increased rapidly, particularly on the multisector CDO desk. Profit margins—the difference between the unit's revenue and what it costs to operate the firm—were exceptional. By the measure of one's worth on Wall Street, which is the ability to make money, Cassano was wildly successful.

Prior performance does not determine future performance, however, just as ordinary investors are warned in financial disclaimers. The arc that tracks the price of a stock, bond, or commodity rarely moves up and to the right with ease. Rather, the situational context is constantly shifting, causing the price to jump higher or lower, a little bit or a lot, moment to moment, and as diligently charted on the long arc of its trading.

A decision arc moves the same way, fluctuating with those forces exerted upon it, both controllable and uncontrollable.

Cassano's arc changed as the situational context changed. He led the creation of a beautiful financial machine in the early 2000s. But no longer was FP creating asymmetric value by solving one-off financial conundrums with massive rewards paid. Instead, it was solving one limited problem over and over.[294] FP's DNA changed. The enterprise architecture did not, at least not enough.

The gross margins on these small slices of fees remained high. The way to achieve this was by keeping FP's expenses down, most notably by using few team members in the deals. When the rewards were divvied up among those team members through bonus compensation, the lifeblood of how Wall Street recruits and retains bright minds wrapped within aggressive spirits, fewer slices of the pie were required. Each member would take a large slice. Cassano would take the biggest one. From 2002 to 2005, as the FP machine printed cash, the strategy behind this new moneymaking model was validated. The roots for the fallacy of success were anchoring into the enterprise.

Beginning in 2005, the situational context was shifting. Some began to see it, including Park. The game going forward would be different. New vulnerabilities would be exposed. New opportunities would be created.

The FP desk that wrote contracts for the subprime market was in fact an extraordinarily small team of six or eight people who "touched" a deal. The reality is that as the small, understaffed, and siloed teams of FP processed more and more deals each month to hit revenue and compensation targets, they lost sight of monitoring the risks going into the underlying deals.

There was no time for meaningful diligence.

---

70 Actors must understand the constantly shifting and virtually always unwritten rules of the game. Those opportunities and threats with the most influential effects on the ultimate outcomes very often arise in the subtle shifts apparent to some but not all players in the game.

They were focused on getting as many deals done as fast as possible.

They were blind to the shifts taking place within those deals, including how the underlying asset quality was deteriorating.

They lost sight of understanding how subtle changes in the master agreements could be a trip wire they would later have to face.

They underappreciated how a change to the mark-to-market accounting standard would help create a perfect storm in which default risk quickly became liquidity risk for individual institutions, which in turn could spark systemic risk as more institutions faced simultaneously weakening positions.

But because of their prior, self-validating success, they pushed on.[295]

---

71 An individual's prior success is a poor predicter of their probability of success in a different situational context.

Cassano's successful track record in building a beautiful financial machine from 2002 to 2005 was, however, uncorrelated to his ability to manage the new situational context of 2005 to 2008. His error was not his alone.

The larger AIG organization had also come to rely on what proved to be the fallacy of success.

Dozens of similar banks and financial institutions feeding on the system erred, too.

The entirety of the mortgage market was fueled by thousands of decision makers who committed errors all along.

They were in good company.

The power of the fallacy of success compounds. It sees

the arc before it and works fastidiously to keep pushing the arc up and to the right, stoking a continuing run of success for as long as possible.

The fallacy of success does this by creating a narrative that is acceptable to the majority, the most powerful, or those willing to pay the highest price to dominate a narrative that serves their interests.

It then competes with alternative viewpoints, the contrarians, and the dissenters to attain and maintain the dominant view. It fuels the inertia within the course charted by a decision arc.

Common Wisdom

The fallacy of common wisdom is also borne of success. It is rational to embrace. It makes sense. It is often right, which reinforces our reliance upon it to define what we are seeing now and what we can anticipate in the future. It creates cognitive shortcuts. Our assessments and decision-making become more efficient, requiring less time and less energy. Our brain favors it. It roots down into our primal amygdala, sensitizing and desensitizing us to what we will perceive as threats and preconditioning how we will react to those threats. It then rises up into our higher orders of consciousness, shaping our executive and creative functions to create the predominating patterns upon which we build our mental frameworks.

At the same time, anchoring our decision making to the common wisdom creates points of resistance or cognitive fric-

---

72 The common wisdom is a prevailing narrative by the powers most influential to an unfolding decision arc. It is often proven wrong in crucible moments.

---

tion in our minds. To deviate from the common wisdom may require us to stand out, dissent, be rebellious, or risk being outcast. In this way, the common wisdom works to smother alternative viewpoints, limit creativity, and stifle thinking about problems through different frameworks and filters.

The common wisdom is a highly prized commodity. With ownership comes privilege. Those who successfully shape the narrative can control how money flows. They can influence how power is allocated. They can increase the probability of manifesting their envisioned future. They set the pins for the future they imagine.

Banks, for example, hire economists who issue pronouncements on where the economy is headed. As a result, their pronouncements help influence where money flows and from where it will recede. Political parties use pollsters to assess the mood of the public on issues or candidates. While doing so, they structure their queries and methods in ways that shape the narrative most favorably to their cause or candidate. Their objective is to create a perceived common wisdom that resonates with their supporters, reduces the level of cognitive effort required to accept the proposition, eliminates the cognitive friction required to consider alternative views and values, and ultimately casts a vote in favor of the politician. Regulators charged with supervising massive swaths of the economy fight to create narratives that justify what they allow, where they look, and what they stymie or push into the regulated confines of permissibility. If they control the common wisdom, they control the direction of the boat.

Those who control the common wisdom control power.

In the spring of 1998, for example, more than ten years before the global economy came to its brink, the President's Working Group on Financial Markets convened. Alan Greenspan was there, along with Robert Rubin, the former chair of Goldman Sachs and then secretary of the Treasury. Arthur Levitt Jr., the chair of the US Securities and Exchange Commission, was present, as well as Brooksley Born, the chair of the Commodity Futures Trading Commission.

Born had been sounding a warning cry among the illuminati of the financial world. She was concerned about the potential risks lurking beneath the waterline of the derivatives market. It was an exciting creature, but its risks were unknown, and the size of the market was growing exponentially. There was little to no regulation of the market. The regulators had little visibility into the size of the market or its growing diversity of instruments. In a zero-sum world like finance, where one gambler's gain is realized from another's loss, it was feared that derivatives trading was a game of the innovative and sophisticated against the vulnerable and the dupes. Born warned this growing, unregulated market posed a significant systemic risk to the larger financial system. In short, she warned that if these new dark markets of immense scale were significantly disrupted, a cascading series of adverse effects could quickly spread through the greater financial system.[296]

The three wisemen—Greenspan, Rubin, and Levitt[297]—told Born to back off.[298]

Subsequently, in 2003, now two years before the credit derivatives markets began to quiver—and five years before it would reach the brink of implosion—the world's central bankers convened at a lodge in Grand Teton National Park near Jackson Hole, Wyoming. Greenspan was there again, as was Ben Bernanke, then a sitting member of the Federal Reserve Board of Governors, along with the president of the European Central Bank and the governor of the Bank of England, among others.

Raghuram Rajan, on leave from the University of Chicago's business school while acting as the chief economist of the International Monetary Fund, was at the conference to present a paper. He posited that financial executives were gambling in the derivatives markets to secure short-term gains, but in a way that could have disastrous consequences to the greater financial system if there was a significant adverse event. Afterward, Lawrence Summers, a former secretary of the Treasury and president of Harvard University, called Rajan a "Luddite" for his views.[299] Other academics who urged caution during this period were similarly ostracized or panned for their views. The wizened mandarins established the common wisdom. The views of others were quelled.

The common wisdom proved wrong.

🔢 Dissent is a powerful agent for improving decision-making. It is often misused, misread, or disregarded.

Similar dynamics occurred during the Global War on Terrorism. In France, over the course of the year leading up to the 2015 Paris terrorist attacks, there were several smaller ones. A common thread ran through these prior events: the victims were Jewish. As a consequence, the common wisdom that emerged within the French national security community, working to build the patterns it would observe and pursue, was that future attacks would likely be against other Jewish businesses or individuals. This presumption colored their surveillance. When the later attacks occurred in September 2015, they did not target French Jews.[300] The common wisdom was incorrect, and it left the French national security apparatus scrambling to quickly establish new filters to understand the purpose, motivations, and techniques of the attacks.

Simultaneously, within the United States' national security apparatus, the common wisdom emerging prior to 2015 was that the next terrorist threats would likely be by a lone wolf. The thinking was that the terrorist networks during this period lacked the sophistication and capital to meaningfully organize a large-scale attack on American or European targets. Instead, they would launch micro attacks, killing or wounding a small number of people, garnering a measure of media attention for their cause or plight, and then be killed or incapacitated. This common wisdom held by the mandarins of US national security also proved wrong.[301]

The French attacks were in fact executed by a highly orchestrated team, seemingly well trained and working in concert to sow fear and destruction across the city.[302] Perhaps because of the incorrect common wisdom in France and the United States, national security teams looked in the wrong places. What resulted led to the most significant acts of carnage in France since the end of WWII.

Working further backward to the early 1980s, as the balance of Cold War power ebbed and flowed between the United States and the Soviet Union, US intelligence experts knew that the Soviets were developing a new class of submarines that would become known as the Akula. They anticipated it would take the Soviets ten years to deliver these vessels to the sea. There would be time to react. Instead, it took only three years for the Soviets to bring their newest nuclear boat to the waters. The established narrative was wrong. Judgment would be invoked much sooner than anticipated.

Fallacy of Ideology

Controlling, influencing, or seeking to shape the group narrative can manifest a third fallacy that leads to errors in decision-making in crucible moments. This is the fallacy of ideology. Ideology is irrelevant in crucible moments of decision-making, as are the philosophies, tropes, memes, and games that go with it.

Within hours of the Paris bombings, for example, talking heads emerged on the major networks to criticize Obama's strategy in the Global War on Terror. Their criticisms included that the bombings would be used to make the case that Democrats were too weak to steward the country's national security policy. The critique would play into a traditional trope used by Republicans to drive differentiation in the minds of voters—namely, that Democrats were weak on terrorism, military strategy, foreign policy, law enforcement, immigration, or any number of security issues.

The strategy had previously proven effective when Ronald Reagan used Jimmy Carter's perceived weakness to win an election. In 1988, Democratic presidential candidate Michael Dukakis's campaign imploded after a photo ran in newspapers where he looked like a man masquerading as a little boy in an army tank. This also fueled the perception that a Democratic candidate was not tough enough to lead the nation's military strategy. Republican commentators would seek to portray Obama as similarly weak.

The reality is that in the moment in which the White House Situation Room and other national security departments are

---

🔢 Ideology is meaningless to success when the stakes are the greatest.

---

scrambling, there is no room for ideological battles. The mission, and getting the decisions right, becomes imperative.

As another illustration of the fallacy of ideology, a Republican appointee, as the chair of the US Federal Reserve, took a laissez-faire approach to the dark markets in the decade-long run-up to the 2008 financial crisis. This approach is consistent with traditional Republican orientation toward free market capitalism, keeping government oversight or regulation tightly constrained. In the end, however, a full-scale global economic implosion was headed off by a government-led, taxpayer-financed resolution designed and executed by a Republican appointee as president of the Federal Reserve Board of New York (Geithner), a Republican-appointed secretary of the Treasury (Henry Paulson), a Republican-appointed Federal Reserve Board of Governors chair (Bernanke) and a Republican president (George W. Bush). In a crucible moment, the ideological leanings of these key decision makers were irrelevant to solving the crisis at hand.[303]

The Silent Stewards of Judgment

Mission-oriented leaders are hard to find. By subverting their *I* in service to the *we*, they slip from the attention-generating tactics of those who seek the light of media, public recognition, and being the story unto themselves.

Instead, mission-oriented leaders are most often the silent stewards who toil behind the scenes, just beyond where the media and stargazers look. They prepare the soil for the decision that inevitably must be made.

Brooks worked well out of the public eye to ensure the United States' decision-making apparatus for managing national security threats was high-functioning and ever-improving. She remains deeply involved in the US defense and national security communities.

Hack, the submarine commander, spent the entirety of his military career in the Silent Service, as the submarine forces of the US Navy are called, working in ways never known to the public or the enemy, all in service to a nation seeking to avert global conflict and nuclear war. He was awarded the Navy Distinguished Service Medal for exceptional meritorious service. The USS *Guardfish* was decommissioned in 1992. The Akula (K-263) was decommissioned in 2011. Today, American nuclear submariners continue to battle for advantage under the sea. Hack has continued to advise them on how.

One would know Robinson only as one of the individuals observed on C-SPAN whispering instructions and handing scripts to the presiding officer of the House of Representatives or the Senate, seemingly the true steward over the fractious, chaotic, and tedious yet highly structured floor debates. Yet he would be anonymous to nearly all others. His sole purpose was to ensure the most important policy debates of a nation were conducted well.

Liebergall stayed on with AIG for another eight years following the worst of the financial crisis. He helped rebuild the company. "I felt a responsibility," he said. "It is where I needed to be." He was part of what is now regarded as one of the greatest corporate turnarounds in US history.

These are several of the silent stewards of great decisions upon which sound judgment has depended when it mattered most.

Indicators

There are seven indicators that help reveal the probable path of an unfolding decision arc. The path is not random.

---

75 Certain indicators help reveal how judgment will be exercised in a crucible moment, thereby increasing our ability to forecast the path of a decision arc and the moves of the actors.

It should not be a surprise. It should not be subjective or left to gut reactions. Instead, a player should be able to assess, manage, and navigate the path in a manner to increase the decision maker's probability of success.

These seven indicators determine if the arc will rise or fall. By understanding their independent influence upon the path of the decision arc, as well as their cross-correlations, it is possible to better understand the biases, proclivities, and patterns for how the players in the game will make their next set of decisions. This understanding can be leveraged to create advantage—ideally, asymmetric advantage. Alternative courses of action can be sketched. Probabilities can be assigned to alternative potential paths. The focus, energy, and resources of the leader and team can be aligned to gain maximum advantage.

What results is that the player best using the emerging calculus involving the indicators, the one who is able to knit together a strategy for managing the interplay between them and who can best forecast how judgment will be exercised by the competing players, will win. The USS *Guardfish* will be able to move itself up under the belly of the Akula. Goldman Sachs will be able to place its first capital call on AIG FP, setting in motion a series of falling dominoes. Hollande can lock down a stadium full of fans to protect them rather than letting them unwittingly run toward their own slaughter.

Agitation

The first indicator is *agitation*. Static environments reveal little. Agitated environments enable the deeper codes in a decision arc to be better revealed.

76 Agitated environments reveal decision-making archetypes with the greatest clarity.

Agitation increases uncertainty and conflict. Perception and cognition may be impaired. New stimuli and new connections emerge. The emotional patterns of individuals and teams become highly sensitized. Bad behaviors will be exhibited. Discipline can be shaken. Fear runs just below the surface. Sometimes it will tear across the top of it.

Agitated environments should not be avoided but instead sought. They create action, friction, shifts, change, and pressure, all of which are revelatory to our understanding of the decision arc and improving our forecasted path ahead.

77 Effective decision-making requires a deft understanding of the unique behaviors and dynamics within the present situational context.

As an example of agitation at work and why to look for it, there were indications that the bloom was off the rose in the subprime credit market in late 2006 and early 2007. Market participants were getting nervous, some more than others. Park was waving his arms inside of AIG FP. Cassano told him to stand down. In the several years prior, the growth of the market had been astounding, with the supply chain for subprime instruments growing exponentially. The financial charts moved to the right and up quarter over quarter, month over month. Many hoped this would never change. As the trajectory of the line on the chart started to bob and weave in the conflicting forecasts regarding what lie ahead, the players with positions in the game started to fracture.

For some, the agitation was a signal—a precondition for opportunity. As author Michael Lewis described in the 2010 book *The Big Short: Inside the Doomsday Machine*, obscure hunters in the financial markets were lurking just outside the mainstream waters of the subprime credit derivatives market, metaphorically positioned much like the USS *Guardfish* lurking in the darkened waters off Vladivostok, waiting for the opportunity to strike.

Agitation was a cue that the truth would soon be revealed, even if it had to be discovered through the difficult journey of friction, confusion, and loss.

It signaled there would be movement soon.

Winners would be crowned. Those who missed the cue, or who could not find a way to change their path, would lose.

The short sellers sensed opportunity. They would harvest billions in profits.

Agitation can be a perceptual reality, where the target is fighting within the context of a noisy environment filled with conflicting, disparate, unorganized, energetically charged, and manipulated information. It is overwhelming, and it taxes the target's ability to analyze, organize, or prioritize the information in a manner that leads to rational decision-making. It obscures the path of the arc. The political debates that Robinson studied, for example, thrashed about in highly charged environments. Here, separating the real from the faux—whether it be news, public sentiment, or true public needs surrounding economic, social, security, or other issues—is extremely difficult. There are interests that benefit from the confusion. The intentional agitation of an environment creates an opportunity to bend the arc. The line between rationality and irrationality is blurred. When the leaders are unable to sort the signal from the noise and find the truth in rational decision-making, we witness crises that should have otherwise been avoidable, as well as opportunities, such as the 2008 financial crisis and the short sellers' actions.

Agitation can also manifest as a physical reality. The terrorists who orchestrated the 2015 Paris attacks used the variable of agitation in a different way. They used it to change the physical environment, using suicide bombers strapped with TATP-laced vests and shooters racing across the city in ordinary black sedans that blended into the traffic to inject fear and terror into the populace. This amplified the chaos and confusion, taxing the individual and collective brains of French citizens and first responders. The agitation of bombs and gunfire, blood and death, was a means for revealing the weak spots in the French security apparatus. If successful, this would reveal the soft underbelly of Paris, and the terrorists ostensibly could strike an even more catastrophic blow, David finding a path for slaying their Goliath—a triumph in the use of the asymmetric power by the little guy against the formidable state.

Similarly, Hack and the crew of the USS *Guardfish* exploited the physical reality of the Akula's agitated environment. The new Akula was in its sea trials. A Soviet commander on the other side of the gambit was aboard a new vessel. The crew was still learning. Their attention was focused on finding problems. Boats leak. Machines fail. Circuits blow. Men stumble. It is noisy, as the machine is pushed to its upper limits to force it to reveal its weaknesses and breakpoints. The noisy environment inside the new Akula kept their attention focused within the vessel rather than on the threats that lay outside.

Agitation made them vulnerable.

Objective Position

The second indicator is the influence of the conditions that reveal one's *objective position* along an unfolding decision arc. The objective position is the true position of the player relative to all others in the game in this moment. For a politician, this may be the strength of their mandate. Their mandate may stem from electoral sentiment, particularly on the heels of a strong election or a weak one. Their mandate also may spring from the present situational context, as in the case of Hollande, who received his the moment the first bomb exploded at the stadium.

For a business leader, it may be the strength or weakness of their financial position, growth rate, or market share rel-

---

78 The objective position of a player in the game is revealed by their position relative to the decision arc, the shifting conditions, and the competitors.

---

ative to others. The bank executives convened by Geithner in September 2008 to find a solution to the gathering storm continuously tested the strength of their own balance sheets, including the strengths or weaknesses of their cash positions, the enduring value of their assets, their short-term liabilities coming due in the next several days and weeks, and their exposure to the risk that a counterparty might fail and drag them under as well. They were testing the strength of their objective position in the game.

In moments like these, the player may have greater or lesser strength to advance their objective relative to the other players. Understanding this objective position then shapes judgment as the optimal path forward.

Leverage

The third indicator is *leverage*. Players look for ways in which they can force others to act or react so that they may gain leverage.[304] Geithner sought to stake out the early ground

---

79 Possession of leverage along the decision arc, including its strengthening or weakening relative to others, determines the ebbing power of the player to shape the decision outcome.

---

for shaping a bank-led solution to the crisis. He came from a position of perceived strength as the head of the Federal Reserve Bank of New York. The banks then patiently waited. As the crisis continued to escalate, Geithner's leverage over the banks was revealed to be actually quite low. Because he was unwilling to provide any financial guaranties or put other government funds at risk to stanch the crisis, his power was merely in holding the bully pulpit.

As time passed, the crisis intensified. Geithner's power gained through rhetoric receded while the banks' power through real or perceived leverage increased. The banks simply waited as their leverage to force the path of the decision arc improved in their favor. It was a gamble for the banks. It worked. A government-led, taxpayer-financed solution became the only viable approach. Geithner was forced to arrange the government bailout.

Time

The passage of *time* is the fourth indicator to deciphering the path of a decision arc and one of the most important. As the clock winds down on a crucible moment, the waning days, hours, and seconds can shift power quickly among the players in the game, redistributing the allocation of leverage among them.

Time was a critical variable in the decision arcs emanating from the Paris attacks. On the night of the bombings, Hollande faced an immediate crisis. Terrorists were actively killing the innocent. The short time on the clock gave him the leverage to act immediately. His authority increased, and he could set the arc. The city was immediately locked down. Civil liberties were suspended. French military strikes on targets in Syria would happen within a day.[305]

Simultaneously, the White House Situation Room was racing to assess the situation as it pertained to American interests. In effect, their analysis was focused on determining

---

80 How well a player manages the amount of time on the clock of the decision arc will often determine both the probability of success and the outcome.

---

the time on their clock. If Americans were also attacked by these terrorists, time would be short. Obama would have to move quickly. He would immediately be vested with a mandate to levy appropriate protective responses as well as retribution for the attacks on Americans. He would have the leverage to move without congressional authority. He could ignore the vocal opponents that would soon stoke the fires on FOX News. The attacks, however, were not directed specifically against American interests. The clock was longer. Accordingly, Obama's response was more measured, as he had less license or necessity to force an immediate decision. In the correlation between time and leverage, he was offered less. He would take more time to do fact-finding and deliberate.

The limitation in the license does something else that is powerful. It permits the opportunity to improve the probability of success in the decision-making by improving the analytical opportunity and enabling a response in which the action is better calibrated to the cause and objective.

Transparency

T he fifth indicator as the stormwaters rise is an ever more *transparent* understanding of the decision archetype of the players involved. These underlying hardwired codes are best revealed when the storm clouds grow angry, and even more so when the waters begin to thrash.

---

81 Once decision archetypes are reliably revealed, the probability of success among the competing actors becomes known.

In the days leading up to the worst moments of the financial crisis, for example, the banks were forced to reveal their paramount desires in protecting their self-interests.

The health of the greater financial system was a secondary priority.

An even more remote concern was the implications for US taxpayers and the fate of the global economy. Service to the *I* was overpowering service to the *we*.

With these priorities now revealed as the crisis intensified, the behaviors of the competing decision archetypes of the players became transparent.

Shifting Rules

The sixth indicator is when the *rules of the game shift* or are suspended. The Fed, for example, maintained early in the crisis that it lacked legal authority to act in emergencies like the one unfolding before it, according to Geithner and the Fed's lawyers. It could not force healthy financial institutions to do something, and it could not directly intervene. By the fourth day of the crisis, however, the rules of the game changed.

---

82 When the rules of the game are uncertain, suspended, or changed, the future path of the decision arc is likely dramatically altered.

The Fed, the Treasury, and Congress had to act, regardless of their statutory authority. The lack of emergency powers under the Federal Reserve Act was deemed an impediment no longer worth worrying about. It had been subsumed by the threat of the crisis. The Fed, the Treasury, and Congress simply had to act regardless of the previously purported rules of the game. Necessity dictated there would be new rules now. A taxpayer-financed bailout was initiated.

With the rules now changed, the surviving banks incurred no losses. They were made fully whole on their positions.

Some even gained. The storm lifted, the river returned to its banks, and the truth was revealed about the power of the players, their motivations, their techniques, and how their respective decision arcs unfolded.

In the Cold War fight below the seas, the United States kept tabs on the Soviet submarine fleet through technology and techniques that worked at a distance. The United States was able to use sonar, eavesdropping, and long-range surveillance, allowing it to remain hidden to the Soviets. When these advantages were lost due to several spy scandals and the Soviets' technological advancements, the United States was forced to get physically closer to Soviet submarines. The rules changed. They would have to get in their 'knickers'. The increasing intensity of the conflict between the superpowers required it.

Fear

The seventh variable in the calculus is the power of *fear*. Decision-making does not occur in antiseptic environments.

▣ Fear is the primal emotion that underpins all decision-making.

It is not a merely intellectual or logical exercise. It is complex and nuanced. Underpinning all decision-making is the most primal of emotions and reactions, either exhibiting itself consciously or pulling the knobs and levers subconsciously. This is fear.

It goes further. Not only does fear influence or drive the individual decision-maker, it can also gain its own life, coursing through populations and systems. It can rage uncontrollably within any player. It will pull at the red-and-black wires of whatever game is being played. As such, it changes the decision arc, sometimes a little and sometimes a lot.

No one could control, for example, the fear spreading through the financial system as the intensity of the crisis increased in 2008. Of the some forty-four thousand contracts to which FP was a party at the time of the bailout, only 125 had subprime exposures.[306] Of this group, it was legitimately argued by both Cassano[307] and Hank[308] that there were no losses, and certainly no material losses in the grand scheme. In other words, AIG's credit derivative exposure did not blow up. It was not the pulse that set off a string of cascading defaults that could not be stopped. Instead, it was fear that caused the markets to spiral. This fear was disconnected from the objective realities of the moment. Fear took on a life of its own. It came to dictate the rules of the game.

Fear was also the operative agent in the Paris attacks, but it was leveraged in a different way. Terrorists create fear to give themselves power in the moment. It enables them to compete with much more powerful fighting forces and countries. It may force opposing decision makers to make an error in managing a new and uncertain decision arc. The error amplifies vulnerabilities that can then be exploited.

Fear also can cause innocent victims to react in unthinking ways. It seemed the Paris terrorists were trying to push panicked soccer fans unknowingly into a second blast zone as they ran from the stadium toward secondary suicide bombers standing just outside the exits. If the strategy worked, they would kill dozens, hundreds, or even thousands more.

Overcoming Irrationality

The first impulse of the human brain when threatened is to fight or flee.

The second impulse is emotional. Our mind and body flashes with anger, fear, and then a desire for retribution.

The third impulse is to rationalize what has happened. It is not possible.

Understanding the mind of a suicide bomber who is willing to strap an unstable cocktail likely made in the kitchen sink of an apartment building with nothing more than bleach and nail polish (rendering the highly explosive and unstable TATP), then mixed with nails and ball bearings; walk up to a stranger with their own story of loneliness, aspirations, and a family somewhere, but who on this evening is just trying to make a bit by patting down other fathers, mothers, and kids who've been looking forward to this match for several months now; look that stranger in the eye; step back; and vaporize oneself into the ether of the night air is not possible.[309]

There is no answer that will satisfy the rational mind. It will not fit into the mental structures we create to understand the world. This is only irrational, falling so far outside the patterns and conventions we erect that the act defies us. It gums up the machinery by which we make rational decisions, which is the point. It is to create fear and uncertainty and, in this moment, opportunity.

This is the reality faced by Hollande and the French first responders. Intentional irrationality is a great leveler among unequal powers. It complicates the calculations on how best to respond. It reduces our ability to anticipate what comes next. It doesn't fit the patterns that the rational mind builds to make sense of the world or our role within it. This is why terrorist organizations spawn suicide bombers. It maximizes chaos. It is unpredictable. It expresses a momentary, uneven advantage in power in their favor that cannot be matched by an aircraft carrier trolling in the Mediterranean Sea, a French Dassault Mirage 2000 screaming across the desert, or a vigilant police officer on a Parisian street unholstering a SIG Sauer. It strikes fear and panic into the populace. It is also the trophy that bolsters fundraising for the cause and recruiting among the disaffected, their portal into the ranks of terrorism.[310] It is merely a piece of the puzzle to spawn and sustain radicalization.

The strategy of brazen, irrational violence is a form of cognitive warfare, designed to increase chaos, panic, fear, emotional overload, and irrational responses among those attacked. It is designed to force decision-making errors by an opponent, revealing small windows where it is possible for their David to harm the Goliath of their narrative.

The defense to cognitive warfare is preparation, discipline, and process. Hollande and the French came to understand this reality quickly. Their adherence to a game plan designed to implement rational decisions and action when the pressures for irrationality were immense could determine whether they saved thousands of lives or lost them. In this moment, they faced their first point of judgment that would set the arc.

Their judgment depended on it.

The Seven Indicators

Leaders can better assess and manage decision arcs by plotting the seven indicators against the following axes:

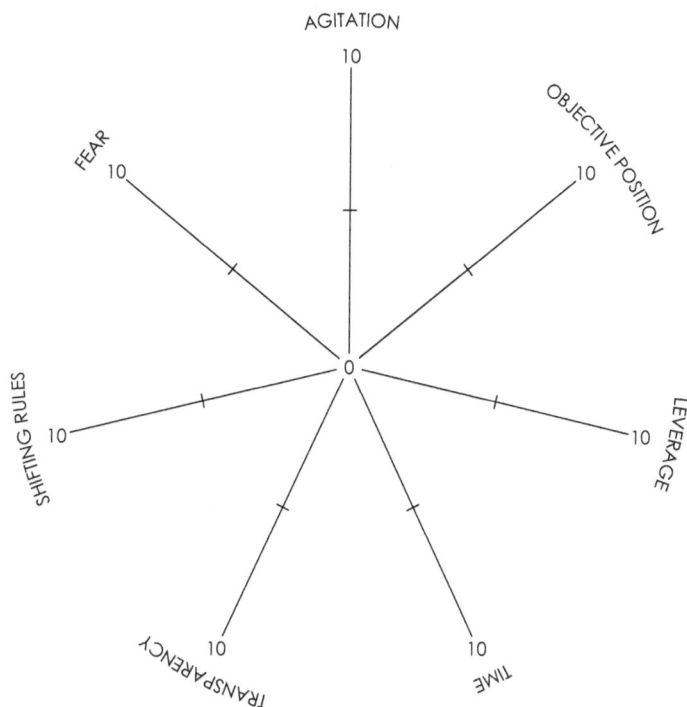

For each indicator, plot its current state, with 10 indicating high levels being experienced or understood. Then use the lessons, methods, and techniques set forth in this book to craft strategies for best managing the decision arc you face, managing each axis to improve your relative position and competitiveness in whatever Darwinian game is before you. By decoding a decision arc in this fashion, a leader's probability of success in their exercise of judgment will be significantly enhanced.

Relentless Self-Flagellation

Adm. Rickover focused on enabling innovative, rebellious, nontraditional thinking to break through barriers.

Rickover was abrasive and off-putting to the institutions that sought authority over development of the US nuclear navy. He, however, charted his own path, moving the nation, the military, and Congress through the ocean of blindness that lay before him and the hundreds of thousands or perhaps millions of people who individually contributed to the creation of the most decisive naval threat during the Cold War—the nuclear submarine.

His method was to instill a discipline of constantly pushing to the outer edge of engineering, human performance, and strategy to secure an advantage while simultaneously scouring for the risks, weaknesses, and the subtle errors of judgment that could cede the entirety of this advantage gained within a single moment of error or weakness. Rickover knew that our greatest threats to getting the momentous decision right do not always emerge from what we know or where we think they hide.

Instead, errors and weaknesses emerge from our blind spots.

Rickover's methods for reducing blind spots and preparing submariners for exercising judgment well in their own crucible moments became woven into the DNA of the vast US nuclear navy. When Hack took command of the USS *Guardfish*, he led eighty men who lived and worked in a pressurized steel tube wrapped around a nuclear reactor, submerged in a far-away and darkened ocean, engaged in a cat-and-mouse game against an enemy with lethal capabilities and uncertain intentions. His success would not be determined by superior engineering, however, for the enemy had likely gained advantage over his Thresher-class submarine with the launch of its Akula. His success also would not be found in the collective firepower and force of the US Navy, as he would execute his most daring missions in absolute silence from all others. Instead, Hack's success in his most critical moment would be found in optimizing the processes and methods for managing his vessel under an array of conditions, threats, and crises.

At an even deeper level, Hack's success or failure would root in the cognitive, emotional, and behavioral intelligence of the eighty men aboard, from the chiefs down through the cooks in the mess, which collectively established the team that could perform at the highest level in the most critical moments.

Hack's management methodology centered on requiring "relentless self-flagellation" by each of the men on his team. They were to learn, practice, and teach, constantly honing their skills until they were nearly automatic, increasing their probability of success when they were later called upon to exercise judgment in their own critical moment. Hack had adapted Rickover's imprint and integrated it into his own managerial command.

Hack's principle of relentless self-flagellation is to embrace self-improvement as a purpose, in part as a method for transcending the ego and self-constructed narratives of each individual sailor within their own minds. The *I* becomes part of the *we*, a transference essential to the success of teams that inevitably face crucible moments. Through the process, the individual's self-awareness of their own capabilities and blind spots becomes attenuated. They come to ask themselves over and over what it is that they are not seeing and where they can improve.

---

84 **The pressures of reacting to an unfolding decision arc can attenuate physical perceptions and emotions. The ability to precondition and manage such dynamics to achieve optimal decision-making creates advantage for the decision maker and the enterprise.**

The process then enables each individual to become aware of the other team members' capacities and weaknesses. This enables the melding together of a team structure premised upon mutual awareness of individual and collective capacities. As trust in these capabilities rises, it is able to later perform at extremely high levels under extremely challenging conditions.

Hack and his officers created the conditions for brutal honesty, compassionate self-improvement, and the collective trust in each man on board in the darkened waters to make the right decisions asked of them when it would count the most.

Their trust had been earned through relentless self-flagellation, optimizing their capabilities while mitigating their blind spots. Because of this preparation, when the Akula was vulnerable, it was a go for Hack and the USS *Guardfish*.

Shape of the Table

The team staffing the White House Situation Room continues to monitor the Paris attacks over the course of the night. Sometime early Saturday morning, Obama's national security adviser sends a memo to Brooks.

The memo provides a seating chart. A large conference room in the White House Situation Room will be used by Obama, his national security adviser, and senior members of the broader community of national security, intelligence, and military departments that collectively interpret the common fact pattern that has been assembled. The implications of the attacks on American interests will be debated. The participants will try to anticipate the likely course of events in the hours, days, and months ahead. They will then establish probabilities of success for alternative courses of action by the United States, including militarily and diplomatically.

---

85 How a decision maker receives information, including the persons, layout, and mode of the communication, has a significant influence on the decision-making process and the ultimate outcome.

The seating chart the national security adviser provides is extraordinarily influential to the tone, tenor, and success of the forthcoming debate. It may even determine the decision. The seating chart quite literally establishes the physical layout for who speaks when, thereby indicating who has priority in the debate and who does not. Those at the conference table have the most influence. Those assigned a seat in the second row of chairs arrayed along the walls of the conference room are secondary. Relative placement on the seating chart sends a first signal for how the national security adviser establishes priorities for the response. If the Department of Defense representatives are closest to the president, the military views and a possible military response are given priority. If the State Department is closest, a diplomatic response is given first priority. If the CIA is given strong positioning, an intelligence response is likely. Participants wrangle for better positioning. It is part of the subtle and sometimes not-so-subtle gamesmanship that goes on among individuals and agencies competing for power in the nation's capital.

An administration's ability to get these decisions right so that the United States can quickly understand, tamp down, or attack the never-ending string of hot spots will often become either a president's greatest moment or greatest failing. When the power and influence in the seating chart are not calibrated to the issue at hand, the debate can quickly become sidetracked. The probability of getting the security decision right by accurately addressing the threats to the nation is lowered. His or her presidential capital will ebb and flow in direct proportion to the success of this decision-making function.

The physical shape of the table and the actual seating chart in the White House Situation Room literally influences the quality of the decision-making and, most likely, the outcome. In this case, the shape of the table reflects a physical layout. In other contexts, this shape is more figurative. In Geithner's management of the financial crisis in 2008, for instance, the interplay of perception, influence, and power in the forthcoming debate was no less determinative to the decision's outcome.

On that Friday night in 2008 when Geithner convened a dozen or so major bank executives at the Fed in Lower Manhattan, he did so within the context of two major financial institutions facing immediate implosion. These early implosions risked setting off a cascade of others, collectively spinning the global financial system into a cataclysmic decline the likes of which had not been seen since the Great Depression. The time on the clock was short. The stakes were immense.

Each of the players convened to participate in this debate had their own leadership archetypes, with worldviews and values that made them extraordinarily successful in the world of global finance. They were expert at the zero-sum nature of the game. They were expert in the hand-to-hand combat of negotiating deals.

Working well on a collective basis, however, was not their strong suit. Given these conditions and players, a pyramidical structure to power and decision-making would have the highest probability of success. This structure could move toward a definitive solution, by hook or by crook, the fastest. To execute this model, the Fed and the Treasury would take the position of the tribal king at the top of the pyramid, and then force, cajole, leverage, or mandate that the powerful chieftains in this greater tribe lay down their arms for the moment and come together for the greater good of the tribe. It was the governance model that Hank had used successfully for over forty years at the helm of AIG.

Geithner, however, lacked the ability to act as the chieftain in a tribal order above all other chieftains.

First, he lacked legal authority to act as the powerful king at the top of a hierarchical order. The Federal Reserve Act did not provide him with the statutory authority to act in this emergency.

Second, the regulators had spent more than a decade purposefully blocking greater transparency or regulation of the derivatives market. Now, as a result, the regulators were blind to the full extent of the risks they faced and how systemic risk might tremor through the global financial system. In short, the king was still fact-finding, trying to raise the anticipated probability of success by fashioning the appropriate remedies for the crisis.

Finally, Geithner and the regulators felt they lacked the political capital to structure a government bailout. They had just taken over Fannie Mae and Freddie Mac only several weeks earlier, and Congress, the public, and the media would likely skewer the regulators if their actions smelled of another taxpayer bailout of Wall Street's sins.

Accordingly, Geithner broke the bank executives up into small working groups. The 'shape of the tables' were, quite literally, small circles. Small groups of equally empowered individuals were charged with working together to develop a collaborative solution to avert the impending implosion of Lehman and possibly AIG. Geithner would cajole a bit but could not play king. He did not directly intervene to broker a solution among the chieftains.

The outcome was predictable. The bank executives returned that evening empty-handed. They would return the following morning to reconvene over coffee and orange juice.

Bank executives make decisions when they sense tremendous individual opportunity for their institutions, or alternatively, when they are leveraged by others. Absent these conditions, they will stall, playing defense until the conditions

86 The duration of a decision arc may compress quickly or lengthen indefinitely, thereby affecting the ability of the players to respond, react, or endure.

improve and new windows open. The governance model used by Geithner on this evening was doomed for failure.

The crisis would continue to spiral. Geithner would be flummoxed to find a path forward—that is, until he, too, was so leveraged as to have no other choice of response. Only when the crisis reached its pinnacle would the leverage on the banking regulators force the definitive decision, the institution of a taxpayer-backed bailout. It would happen on a Tuesday, when Geithner and his regulatory peers felt the conditions had changed and they had no other choice.

87 Increasing pressure on the player will help reveal their decision archetype.

Once this decision was made, his hand at last forced, Geithner acted as the king above the tribe of financial sub-chiefs. The solution was imposed upon the hierarchy of the US financial empire in a predictable fashion. The chieftains of the weakest institutions were sacrificed. Those of the strongest institutions continued to rise, their institutions emerging from the zero-sum game of winners and losers even stronger than before the crisis. The underlying codes and the resulting outcomes for making decisions in crucible moments were once again revealed. The worst-imagined cataclysm was averted.

Ritual Sacrifice

There are other cardinal rules at play. For example, those who commit errors of judgment during crucible moments will be sacrificed.

---

88 Those who commit errors of judgment during crucible moments will be sacrificed.

The ritual of sacrifice is messy and imperfect. A thirst for bloodletting easily rises up in the wake of war, violence, or financial loss. Victims want revenge. It is an indiscriminate energy. Left unchecked, it can consume all before it. It has no use for due process. It does not carefully parse the minds of the accused, showing the restraint to punish only those who possessed the intent to harm, defraud, or act reckless toward others. It hunts with abandon, seeking to quench a thirst that rises up from some deeper instinctual or primal place.

In these moments, leaders can make a further choice. They can tap into the thirst, they can agitate it, or they can succumb to it. The choice they make will correspondingly influence the progress of their decision arc, either positively or negatively.

The AIG experience from 2005 to 2009 is a dramatic and public case study in the ritual of sacrifice. In Hank's thirty-eight years at the helm, he had time and time again demonstrated his ability to align his leadership style in the moment to the specific situational context he faced. He was a master of adjusting his decision-making processes and decision archetype, toggling effectively through the different ecosystems of Wall Street; the political culture of Washington, DC; and the diverse political, financial, legal, and cultural domains of the multitude of foreign countries necessary to create a global behemoth.

The rules of the game shifted in the early 2000s. Reforms in corporate governance increased the power of boards of directors over management, with independent directors carrying increasing responsibility for the strategic direction of large, public companies. Reporting standards changed. Spitzer, the aggressive but flawed legal hunter, saw the opportunity to take down the lion. AIG would be Spitzer's trophy, and he exposed Hank's vulnerability in the new situational context. Hank became the personified image of a wealthy financier disconnected from the present reality and willing to cover up a bad financial transaction. In this moment, he was an easy target. The reconstituted board of directors of AIG, now more powerful, under pressure to exercise their new responsibilities, and facing the prospect of an ugly trial and extended public-relations debacle, forced Hank to retire.[311] The lion failed to adapt to the new environment. As is required of the cardinal rule, he was sacrificed.

Cassano was next. Unlike Hank, he was not known to the broader public. Instead, his reputation was in the more walled-off section of Wall Street. His power was gained by winning in the hand-to-hand combat of financial negotiations of this arena. His prowess in one domain, however, left him ill-prepared to meet the threats of a changed environment. Cassano was unable to fight the war that now centered on the broader market's perception of potential liquidity risk and that could be the trigger point for widescale systemic risk spreading across the global financial system.

Fighting in public with regulators and in the court of public opinion were arenas for which Cassano was ill-suited. In fact, his internal coding was such that he would have likely exacerbated the regulators' fears and the public's hostility toward Wall Street.

Furthermore, Cassano had changed the DNA of FP while at the helm. By the time Goldman Sachs placed its capital call in the summer of 2007, FP was no longer the clever hunter that relied on its quirky brainiacs to craft creative solutions

---

89 It is easy to miss shifts in the balance of power created by long arcs. Players overweight the security of their incumbent position, miss clues as to shifting sands beneath them, grow bored, or are distracted by more immediate, higher intensity challenges.

---

to unsolvable problems. It was vulnerable in the new game, unable to redirect that machine to now solve the problem before it. The tables had turned. AIG was now the hunted.[312] Martin Sullivan, Hank's successor, sacrificed Cassano and a handful of his lieutenants on the multisector CDO desk in early 2008.[313]

Sullivan, known as a genial Brit now thrown into primal combat, was sacrificed shortly thereafter. His decision archetype was misaligned with the situational context he inherited. He was unable to improve the trajectory of the decision arc. He was terminated in June 2008.

Sullivan's successor, Robert Willumstad, made it ninety-one days before the Treasury Department sacrificed him as part of the $85 billion bailout package,[314] a measure deemed necessary for Geithner, Bernanke, and Paulson to better sell the bailout to Congress and the public. (Willumstad's sacrifice was less due to a correlation between a mistake in his judgment to the situational context. Rather, his sacrifice was to appease the public's thirst for blood in retribution for the sins of Wall Street. His head was part of the price that would be paid. This is another dimension of the rule of sacrifice.)

In Willumstad's place, the Treasury Department inserted Edward Liddy, a member of Goldman Sachs's board and the former CEO of Allstate Insurance. Liddy sought to heal AIG. He sought to restore the trust of his people. He also knew the ethos of big finance, in which performance and loyalty in the tribe trades on money, the universal commodity Wall Street uses not as mere compensation but as the essential ingredient that defines self-identity and self-worth. Liddy's strategy was admirable. However, it failed miserably.[315]

Liddy's approach of healing AIG, not only with compassion and kind words but by leveraging Wall Street's most prized commodity—significant incentive compensation for those AIG managers rebuilding AIG—clashed violently with another immutable power energized in this moment: the thirst of politicians and the populace for more blood.[316] Nine months later, he would be sacrificed. Liddy's choices told us much about him and the trophy he hunted.

---

90 Misalignment of the decision maker's archetype with the unique situational context presently faced will result in suboptimal or failed decision-making.

In Liddy's place, the Treasury Department recruited Robert Benmosche, the former head of MetLife who had since retired to his winery on the Croatian coast. Benmosche had been watching the AIG affair from afar. His opinions were notoriously unvarnished, and he owned the room when he speaks them. In his first meeting with the remaining FP team, he told them they had been treated wrongly. AIG now had a leader purpose-built for the moment. For the first time in years, and although the path would still be long and hard-fought, there was a knowing in the AIG ranks that there would be an end, and that end would be in success rather than failure. At long last, with kind words internally and tough talk outwardly, Benmosche was able to break the ritualistic cycle that had plagued AIG and its recovery.

The Quiet

Robinson, the parliamentarian and my early mentor, listened each day to the cacophony emanating from the never-ending theater that is politics and policy-making in Washington, DC. He listened for the sounds that were bold and blaring. He listened for the single perfect note that would sometimes pierce through. He felt the noise rise in intensity, and then fall or at times even go quiet, emitting seemingly no sound at all.

His daily habit was to pore through the news, make calls to insiders, and have meetings with the team and clients. Then he would sit, staring through the large panes of glass framing his office into the ether of nothingness above the busy intersection of Connecticut Avenue and M Street Northwest. I imagined he saw every chord in the cacophony emerging from the city as a decision arc uniquely unfolding. Each imagined arc would wave higher or lower, predictably or chaotically, with intensity or subtlety, finding its way.

What Robinson was doing was surveying the competing arcs to predict which would result in action versus frustration or stagnation. He was seeking to sort the signal from the noise.

He would then contemplate the strategies for influencing the arc of his chosen few to move either higher or lower. Competitors sought to bend each arc to their favor and, in doing so, were required to exercise their own best judgment.

Errors of judgment could cripple an arc, flare it, increase its dysfunction, or kill it. Errors often fueled the noise. The media reveled in any failure and ineptitude among the elected and privileged. Interest groups real or manufactured fanned the flames to benefit their own aims, and political opponents sensed an opportunity to nick or kill.

I came to learn something else in this time, something ironic—moments in which judgment is brilliantly exercised are often very quiet. There is little fanfare. Judgment is exercised discreetly. It is behind closed doors and nondisclosure agreements. It serves little interest to others who instead want drama, stasis, and friction.

This is an injustice, of course. We should celebrate exceptional decision-making. The reality is that our society and its institutions, including business, politics, and the media, favor story lines of anger, frustration, inequity, and injustice. Stories of decision-making success are often uneventful. They do not sell news. They do not send voters to the polls. Their lessons are often forgotten in the ensuing quiet.

The story of Benmosche and his team righting AIG in the wake of its bailout, repaying all monies owed to US taxpayers plus interest, was heralded by few on Wall Street, Main Street, or the halls of Congress. It was a momentous achievement. It was, however, a mere blip in the public narrative. Those who had sought to further use the arc of the financial crisis for their own future gains saw little value in celebrating judgment well exercised.

The story of those few hours in which the USS *Guardfish* pursued the Akula from only several meters away, hidden in her shadow, was a closeted secret. The story was inaccessible to but a privileged few who understand how judgment was well exercised in a crucible moment of Cold War history.

The inside story of the decisions made by Hollande and

the French national security forces over several hours of a highly orchestrated terrorist attack is little known beyond the few directly affected by it. The story of their exceptional judgment exercised in a crucible moment was quickly subsumed into the cacophony of the long-running Global War on Terror.

The reality is that evidence of decision arcs managed well often have less visibility and permanence in our consciousness than those managed poorly. They slip into the quiet.

Yet we should know these lessons. We should strive to sort the signal from the noise. We should listen for the single pure note that is hidden within the blare of discordant notes emerging from the cacophony. We should hunt to resolve errors, inequities, and injustices until we achieve the quiet.

For those who do come to exercise judgment well, who carefully curate its execution, and who render a decision that improves the arc of the decision, expect few accolades. You will, however, be welcomed into an elite *fraternité*—the silent stewards of judgment.

Judgment Mind Map

The purpose of *Judgment: The Art of Momentous Decision-Making* is to draw out the clues, strategies, methods, and techniques that can be used to improve a leader's judgment in their most critical moments, all of which can be downloaded in this mind map:

chrismailander.com/judgmentmindmap

This mind map can be a useful tool for an individual and a team as they plan, develop playbooks, anticipate what will come next, and plot their strategies against both the short and long decision arcs they face in their own unique experiences.

Bibliography

Nuclear Brinkmanship in the Cold War, 1986

in order of first reference

Richard Halloran, "A Silent Battle Surfaces," *The New York Times*, December 7, 1986.

Gary Wetzel, "How the Soviet Akula Changed Submarine Warfare," *Jalopnik*, October 13, 2017.

Soviet Warfare Trends, US Central Intelligence Agency, March 1985 (sanitized version publicly released October 1999, under the CIA Historical Review Program).

John F. Lehman (US Secretary of the Navy), statement before a US Senate subcommittee of the Committee on Appropriations pertaining to the US Department of Defense Appropriations for Fiscal Year 1986, March 7, 1985.

David Devoss, "Red Hunt: Beneath the Pacific, Two Fleets Engage in a Silent War of Maneuver—The Only Battlefield Where US and Soviet Armed Forces Meet. A Rare View from Inside an Attack Submarine," *The Los Angeles Times Magazine*, April 12, 1987.

Roger Thompson, *Lessons Not Learned: The US Navy's Status Quo Culture* (Annapolis, MD: Naval Institute Press, 2007).

Lt. John Howard, "Fixed Sonar Systems: The History and Future of the Underwater Silent Sentinel," *The Submarine Review*, April 2011.

Owen R. Cote Jr., *The Third Battle: Innovation in the US Navy's Silent Cold War Struggle with Soviet Submarines* (Newport, RI: Naval War College, 2000).

John H. Stein, *Soviet Nuclear-Powered Submarines and Their Propulsion Systems*, memorandum from the deputy director for Operations to the director of Central Intelligence, November 21, 1983; declassified and publicly released June 2017.

"SSN Akula Class (Bars Type 971) Nuclear Submarine," Naval Technology, January 11, 2001, http://naval-technology.com/projects/Akula.

Norman Black, "Navy Battle Group Finishes Secret Cruise Off Soviet Coast," The Associated Press, September 29, 1986.

Matthew Carle, "The Mission Behind Operation Ivy Bells and How It Was Discovered," *Military.com*, 2020, https://www.military.com/history/operation-ivy-bells.html.

Kyle Mizokami, "How a Super-Secret US Navy Submarine Tapped Russia's Underwater Communications Cables," *The National Interest*, June 29, 2017, https://nationalinterest.org/blog/the-buzz/how-super-secret-us-navy-submarine-tapped-russias-underwater-21370.

Soviet Military Power, U.S. Government Printing Office, 2017.

James Kraska, "Putting Your Head in the Tiger's Mouth: Submarine Espionage in Territorial Waters," *Columbia Journal of Transnational Law* 54 (2015).

Robert Beckhusen, "New Documents Reveal How a 1980s Nuclear War Scare Became a Full-Blown Crisis," *WIRED*, May 16, 2013.

Wikipedia, s.v. "Komsomolsk-on-Amur," accessed 2020, https://en.wikipedia.org/wiki/Komsomolsk-on-Amur.

James Robb, "A City Built on the Bones of Prisoners," *A Worker at Large* (blog), August 25, 2016, https://convincingreasons.wordpress.com/2016/08/25/komsomolsk-na-amur-a-city-with-a-past-too-ghastly-to-face/comment-page-1/.

"Submarine Launch Procedures at Komsomol'sk Shipyard Amur 199 (S)," National Photographic Interpretation Center, November 1984; declassified by the US Central Intelligence Agency and publicly released on July 20, 2010.

Wikipedia, s.v. "*Akula*-Class Submarine," accessed 2020, https://en.wikipedia.org/wiki/Akula-class_submarine. The Akula (K-263) was launched May 28, 1986, and commissioned on December 30, 1987.

Wikipedia, s.v. "USS *Guardfish* (SSN-612)," accessed 2020, https://en.wikipedia.org/wiki/USS_Guardfish_(SSN-612).

Paul Forsythe Johnston, "The Taming of the Screw," *Angles & Dangles* (blog), The National Museum of American History, accessed 2020, https://americanhistory.si.edu/subs/anglesdangles/taming.html.

Sebastien Roblin, "Why This Russian 'Stealth' Submarine Is a Major Threat to America," *The National Interest*, September 23, 2019.

The Precipice of Global Economic Collapse, 2008

in order of first reference

The Financial Crisis Inquiry Report: Final Report of the National Commission on the Causes of the Financial and Economic Crisis in the United States, January 2011, 334.

James B. Stewart, "Eight Days: The Battle to Save the American Financial System," *The New Yorker*, September 14, 2009.

Author Interview with Jon Liebergall (October 2020).

The AIG Rescue, Its Impact on Markets, and the Government's Exit Strategy, Congressional Oversight Panel, June 10, 2010, 49.

Interview with Joe Cassano, staff audiotape, Financial Crisis Inquiry Commission, June 25, 2010.

Interview with Gene Park, staff audiotape, Financial Crisis Inquiry Commission, May 18, 2010.

Interview with Alan Frost, staff audiotape, Financial Crisis Inquiry Commission, May 11, 2010.

AIG Transcript of Phone Call Between Andrew Forster and John Liebergal [sic], July 30, 2007.

Interview with Andrew Forster, staff audiotape, Financial Crisis Inquiry Commission, June 23, 2010.

William D. Cohan, "The Fall of AIG: The Untold Story," *Institutional Investor*, April 7, 2010.

Robert O'Harrow Jr. and Brady Dennis, "Downgrades and Downfall," *The Washington Post*, December 31, 2008.

Michael Lewis, "The Man Who Crashed the World," *Vanity Fair*, July 6, 2009, https://www.vanityfair.com/news/2009/08/aig200908.

Edward J. Schoen, "The 2007–2009 Financial Crisis: An Erosion of Ethics: A Case Study," *Journal of Business Ethics*, February 23, 2016.

Interview with Gary Gorton, staff audiotape, Financial Crisis Inquiry Commission, May 11, 2010.

Brady Dennis and Robert O'Harrow Jr., "A Crack in the System," *The Washington Post*, December 30, 2008.

Gretchen Morgenson, "Behind Insurer's Crisis, Blind Eye to a Web of Risk," *The New York Times*, September 27, 2008.

John Cassidy, "The AIG Trial Is a Comedy," *The New Yorker*, September 30, 2014.

Matthew J. Berger, "The Gold Standard: The History of Hank Greenberg and AIG," *Journal of International Business and Law*, 2014.

Jacqueline S. Gold, "Is AIG's Hank Greenberg Next?," CNN/Money, October 27, 2004.

Interview with Maurice "Hank" Greenberg, staff audiotape, Financial Crisis Inquiry Commission, May 19, 2010.

"Goldman Defends Its Collateral Calls to AIG," Reuters, August 2, 2010.

Dealbook, "H. Rodge Cohen: The Trauma Surgeon of Wall Street," *The New York Times*, November 15, 2009.

"Financial Crisis: Review of Federal Reserve System Financial Assistance to American International Group, Inc.," US Government Accountability Office, September 2011.

John Carney, "Here's the Untold Story of How AIG Destroyed Itself," *Business Insider*, March 3, 2010.

Jonathan Kandell, "Beyond the Turnaround at AIG," *Institutional Investor*, November 26, 2012.

Gautam Mukunda and Thomas J. DeLong, "Gerry Pasciucco at AIG Financial Products," *Harvard Business School Publishing*, July 31, 2013.

Robert O'Harrow Jr. and Brady Dennis, "The Beautiful Machine," *The Washington Post*, December 29, 2008.

Wikipedia, s.v. "Maurice R. Greenberg," accessed 2020, https://en.wikipedia.org/wiki/Maurice_R._Greenberg.

Jenny Anderson, "Greenberg and AIG Sever Ties," *The New York Times*, March 29, 2005.

"Hank Greenberg's Exit Marks the End of an Era," *Business Insurance*, March 20, 2005.

Monica Langley, "After a 37-Year Reign at AIG, Chief's Last Tumultuous Days," *The Wall Street Journal*, April 1, 2005.

Carol J. Loomis, "AIG: Aggressive. Inscrutable. Greenberg.," *Fortune*, April 27, 1998.

Robert McDonald and Anna Paulson, *AIG in Hindsight*, Federal Reserve Bank of Chicago, October 2014.

Jake DeSantis, "Dear AIG, I Quit!," *The New York Times*, March 24, 2009.

Jeff Gerth, "In Private Papers, a More Candid Tim Geithner Speaks Out," *ProPublica*, October 30, 2014.

Carol D. Leonnig, "AIG Founder Wielded Personal Influence in Washington," *The Washington Post*, October 1, 2008.

Anthony Faiola, Ellen Nakashima, and Jill Drew, "What Went Wrong," *The Washington Post*, October 15, 2008.

Jackie Northam, "Hitting ISIS Where It Hurts by Striking Oil Trucks," NPR, November 19, 2015.

Email from Gene Park to Joseph Cassano, "CDO of ABS Approach Going Forward—Message to the Dealer Community," February 28, 2006.

Crescendo in the Global War on Terror, 2015

in order of first reference

Tara McKelvey, "The Do's and Don'ts of the Situation Room," BBC, August 13, 2018.

Rachel Donadio, "What the November 13 Attacks Taught Paris," *The Atlantic*, November 13, 2018.

"2015 Paris Terror Attacks Fast Facts," CNN, November 13, 2019.

"Paris Attacks: What Happened on the Night," BBC, December 9, 2015.

"The Attacks on Paris: Lessons Learned," Homeland Security Advisory Council and the Paris Public Safety Delegation, June 2016.

Mariano Casillo, Margot Haddad, Michael Martinez, and Steve Almasy, "Paris Suicide Bomber Identified; ISIS Claims Responsibility for 129 Dead," CNN, November 16, 2015.

Peter Baker and Eric Schmitt, "Paris Terror Attacks May Prompt More Aggressive US Strategy on ISIS," *The New York Times*, November 14, 2015.

Wikipedia, s.v. "Situation Room," accessed 2020, https://en.wikipedia.org/wiki/Situation_Room.

"Paris Terror Attacks: France Launches Fresh Airstrikes on ISIS in Syria— As It Happened," *The Guardian*, November 17, 2015, updated April 14, 2018.

Ken Johnson, "Situation: Ambiguous," *The New York Times*, May 7, 2011.

Wikipedia, s.v. "November 2015 Paris Attacks," accessed 2020, https://en.wikipedia.org/wiki/November_2015_Paris_attacks.

Michael Donley, Cornelius O'Leary, and John Montgomery, "Inside the White House Situation Room: A National Nerve Center," US Central Intelligence Agency, April 14, 2007.

"President Obama Offers a Statement on the Attacks in Paris," The White House, November 13, 2015.

Aaron David Miller, "Why the Paris Attacks Won't Be a Game-Changer for Obama," *Foreign Policy (FP)*, November 18, 2015.

Jose Pagliery, "US Takes Aim at the ISIS Oil Business," CNN, December 11, 2015.

Domenico Montanaro, "US Political Reaction to Paris Attacks Split Along Party Lines," NPR, November 14, 2015.

Michael R. Gordon and Eric Schmitt, "US Steps Up Its Attacks on ISIS-Controlled Oil Fields in Syria," *The New York Times*, November 12, 2015.

Richard Sisk, "US Choice to Drop Leaflets in Syria Contrasts with Russian Way of War," Military.com, November 19, 2015.

Juliet Eilperin and Steven Mufson, "Recent Terrorist Attacks Push Obama to Reassess, and Defend, His Strategy," *The Washington Post*, December 7, 2015.

Robert Burns, "US Says 116 Islamic State Oil Trucks Destroyed in Syria Airstrikes," TPM, November 17, 2015.

Peter Baker and Eric Schmitt, "Paris Terror Attacks May Prompt More Aggressive US Strategy on ISIS," *The New York Times*, November 14, 2015.

Alissa J. Rubin and Anne Barnard, "France Strikes ISIS Targets in Syria in Retaliation for Attacks," *The New York Times*, November 15, 2015.

"Tactics, Techniques, and Procedures Used in the 13 November 2015 Paris Attacks," unclassified, *Joint Intelligence Bulletin*, November 23, 2015.

Trent Elliott, "Complex Coordinated Terrorist Attack: Considerations for Practical Emergency Preparedness and Resiliency Exercises," *Wright State University*, 2017.

Notes

1. Richard Halloran, "A Silent Battle Surfaces," *The New York Times*, December 7, 1986.

2. Gary Wetzel, "How the Soviet Akula Changed Submarine Warfare," *Jalopnik*, October 13, 2017.

3. *Soviet Warfare Trends*, US Central Intelligence Agency, March 1985 (sanitized version publicly released October 1999, under the CIA Historical Review Program).

4. *Soviet Warfare Trends*.

5. Wetzel.

6. *Soviet Warfare Trends*.

7. *Soviet Warfare Trends*.

8. Halloran.

9. *Soviet Warfare Trends*.

10. Halloran.

11. John F. Lehman (US Secretary of the Navy), statement before a US Senate subcommittee of the Committee on Appropriations pertaining to the US Department of Defense Appropriations for Fiscal Year 1986, March 7, 1985.

12. *Soviet Warfare Trends* and Wetzel.

13. David Devoss, "Red Hunt: Beneath the Pacific, Two Fleets Engage in a Silent War of Maneuver—The Only Battlefield Where US and Soviet Armed Forces Meet. A Rare View from Inside an Attack Submarine," *The Los Angeles Times Magazine*, April 12, 1987.

14. *Soviet Warfare Trends* and Wetzel.

15. Roger Thompson, *Lessons Not Learned: The US Navy's Status Quo Culture* (Annapolis, MD: Naval Institute Press, 2007).

16. Thompson.

17. Thompson.

18. Lt. John Howard, "Fixed Sonar Systems: The History and Future of the Underwater Silent Sentinel," *The Submarine Review*, April 2011.

19. Howard.

20. Halloran.

21. Owen R. Cote Jr., *The Third Battle: Innovation in the US Navy's Silent Cold War Struggle with Soviet Submarines* (Newport, RI: Naval War College, 2000).

22. Cote.

23. Cote.

24. John H. Stein, *Soviet Nuclear-Powered Submarines and Their Propulsion Systems*, memorandum from the deputy director for Operations to the director of Central Intelligence, November 21, 1983; declassified and publicly released June 2017.

25. Stein.

26. "SSN Akula Class (Bars Type 971) Nuclear Submarine," Naval Technology, January 11, 2001, http://naval-technology.com/projects/Akula.

27. Cote.

28. Wetzel.

29. Norman Black, "Navy Battle Group Finishes Secret Cruise Off Soviet Coast," The Associated Press, September 29, 1986.

30. Matthew Carle, "The Mission Behind Operation Ivy Bells and How It Was Discovered," *Military.com*, 2020, https://www.military.com/history/operation-ivy-bells.html.

31. Carle. Incidentally, the surveillance device the Americans used in Operation Ivy Bells is on display at the KGB Museum in Moscow.

32. Carle.

33. Kyle Mizokami, "How a Super-Secret US Navy Submarine Tapped Russia's Underwater Communications Cables," *The National Interest*, June 29, 2017, https://nationalinterest.org/blog/the-buzz/how-super-secret-us-navy-submarine-tapped-russias-underwater-21370.

34. *Soviet Military Power*, U.S. Government Printing Office, 2017.

35. James Kraska, "Putting Your Head in the Tiger's Mouth: Submarine Espionage in Territorial Waters," *Columbia Journal of Transnational Law* 54 (2015). Robert Beckhusen, "New Documents Reveal How a 1980s Nuclear War Scare Became a Full-Blown Crisis," WIRED, May 16, 2013.

36. Halloran.

37. Halloran.

38. Wikipedia, s.v. "Komsomolsk-on-Amur," accessed 2020, https://en.wikipedia.org/wiki/Komsomolsk-on-Amur.

39. Wikipedia, s.v. "Komsomolsk-on-Amur."

40. James Robb, "A City Built on the Bones of Prisoners," *A Worker at Large* (blog), August 25, 2016, https://convincingreasons.

wordpress.com/2016/08/25/komsomolsk-na-amur-a-city-with-a-past-too-ghastly-to-face/comment-page-1/.

41. Robb.

42. "Submarine Launch Procedures at Komsomol'sk Shipyard Amur 199 (S)," National Photographic Interpretation Center, November 1984; declassified by the US Central Intelligence Agency and publicly released on July 20, 2010.

43. National Photographic Interpretation Center.

44. National Photographic Interpretation Center.

45. National Photographic Interpretation Center.

46. Wikipedia, s.v. "*Akula*-Class Submarine," accessed 2020, https://en.wikipedia.org/wiki/Akula-class_submarine. The Akula (K-263) was launched May 28, 1986, and commissioned on December 30, 1987.

47. National Photographic Interpretation Center.

48. Wikipedia, s.v. "USS *Guardfish* (SSN-612)," accessed 2020, https://en.wikipedia.org/wiki/USS_Guardfish_(SSN-612).

49. Wikipedia, s.v. "*Akula*-Class Submarine".

50. The USS *Guardfish* (SSN-612) was 279 feet long, or roughly 25 percent smaller than the Akula-I.

51. Wikipedia, s.v. "USS *Guardfish* (SSN-612)".

52. Paul Forsythe Johnston, "The Taming of the Screw," *Angles & Dangles* (blog), The National Museum of American History, accessed 2020, https://americanhistory.si.edu/subs/anglesdangles/taming.html.

53. Sebastien Roblin, "Why This Russian 'Stealth' Submarine Is a Major Threat to America," *The National Interest*, September 23, 2019.

54. Roblin.

55. Roblin.

56. *The Financial Crisis Inquiry Report: Final Report of the National Commission on the Causes of the Financial and Economic Crisis in the United States*, January 2011, 334.

57. James B. Stewart, "Eight Days: The Battle to Save the American Financial System," *The New Yorker*, September 14, 2009.

58. Stewart.

59. Stewart.

60. Stewart.

61. Stewart.

62. Stewart.

63. *The Financial Crisis Inquiry Report*, 345.

64. Author Interview with Jon Liebergall (October 2020).

65. *The AIG Rescue, Its Impact on Markets, and the Government's Exit Strategy*, Congressional Oversight Panel, June 10, 2010, 49.

66. *The Financial Crisis Inquiry Report*, 344.

67. Interview with Joe Cassano, staff audiotape, Financial Crisis Inquiry Commission, June 25, 2010.

68. *The Financial Crisis Inquiry Report*, 266.

69. Interview with Gene Park, staff audiotape, Financial Crisis Inquiry Commission, May 18, 2010.

70. *The Financial Crisis Inquiry Report*, 268.

71. *The Financial Crisis Inquiry Report*, 243–244.

72. *The Financial Crisis Inquiry Report*, 266.

73. Interview with Alan Frost, staff audiotape, Financial Crisis Inquiry Commission, May 11, 2010.

74. AIG Transcript of Phone Call Between Andrew Forster and John Liebergal [sic], July 30, 2007.

75. Interview with Andrew Forster, staff audiotape, Financial Crisis Inquiry Commission, June 23, 2010.

76. *The AIG Rescue, Its Impact on Markets, and the Government's Exit Strategy*, 49.

77. *The Financial Crisis Inquiry Report*, 213.

78. *The Financial Crisis Inquiry Report*, page 129.

79. Interview with Gene Park.

80. *The Financial Crisis Inquiry Report*, 266–267.

81. William D. Cohan, "The Fall of AIG: The Untold Story," *Institutional Investor*, April 7, 2010.

82. Interview with Alan Frost.

83. Interview with Alan Frost.

84. Interview with Gene Park.

85. Interview with Gene Park.

86. Interview with Joe Cassano.

87. Robert O'Harrow Jr. and Brady Dennis, "Downgrades and Downfall," *The Washington Post*, December 31, 2008.

88. Interview with Gene Park.

89. Interview with Gene Park.

90. *The AIG Rescue, Its Impact on Markets, and the Government's Exit Strategy*, 49. Of some forty-four thousand contracts AIG FP was party to at the time of the bailout, only 125 had subprime exposures. Of the more than one hundred thousand AIG employees, only a half dozen or so were directly associated with these 125 contracts.

91. Interview with Alan Frost.

92. Interview with Gene Park.

93. Interview with Andrew Forster.

94. Interview with Andrew Forster.

95. Michael Lewis, "The Man Who Crashed the World," *Vanity Fair*, July 6, 2009, https://www.vanityfair.com/news/2009/08/aig200908.

96. Interview with Gene Park.

97. Interview with Gene Park.

98. Interview with Gene Park.

99. *The Financial Crisis Inquiry Report*, 8. More precisely, the term coined on Wall Street was "IBGYBG," which meant, "I'll be gone; you'll be gone," and referred to the notion that the market participants knew that this market would explode shortly. But until then, they would continue to harvest the fees and disappear before the explosion occurred.

100. *The Financial Crisis Inquiry Report*, 102.

101. *The Financial Crisis Inquiry Report*, xxv.

102. *The Financial Crisis Inquiry Report*, 22.

103. Edward J. Schoen, "The 2007–2009 Financial Crisis: An Erosion of Ethics: A Case Study," *Journal of Business Ethics*, February 23, 2016.

104. *The AIG Rescue, Its Impact on Markets, and the Government's Exit Strategy*, 49.

105. *The Financial Crisis Inquiry Report*, 292.

106. *The Financial Crisis Inquiry Report*, 237.

107. *The Financial Crisis Inquiry Report*, 269.

108. *The Financial Crisis Inquiry Report*, 235.

109. *The Financial Crisis Inquiry Report*, 143.

110. *The Financial Crisis Inquiry Report*, 200, 237.

111. Interview with Gary Gorton, staff audiotape, Financial Crisis Inquiry Commission, May 11, 2010.

112. *The Financial Crisis Inquiry Report*, 266.

113. *The Financial Crisis Inquiry Report*, 266.

114. Lewis.

115. Brady Dennis and Robert O'Harrow Jr., "A Crack in the System," *The Washington Post*, December 30, 2008.

116. Gretchen Morgenson, "Behind Insurer's Crisis, Blind Eye to a Web of Risk," *The New York Times*, September 27, 2008.

117. John Cassidy, "The AIG Trial Is a Comedy," *The New Yorker*, September 30, 2014.

118. Cohan.

119. Matthew J. Berger, "The Gold Standard: The History of Hank Greenberg and AIG," *Journal of International Business and Law*, 2014.

120. Jacqueline S. Gold, "Is AIG's Hank Greenberg Next?," CNN/Money, October 27, 2004.

121. *The AIG Rescue, Its Impact on Markets, and the Government's Exit Strategy*, 49.

122. Interview with Gary Gorton.

123. Interview with Alan Frost.

124. Interview with Gene Park.

125. *The Financial Crisis Inquiry Report*, 244.

126. Interview with Maurice "Hank" Greenberg, staff audiotape, Financial Crisis Inquiry Commission, May 19, 2010.

127. "Goldman Defends Its Collateral Calls to AIG," Reuters, August 2, 2010.

128. *The Financial Crisis Inquiry Report*, 244.

129. Interview with Joe Cassano.

130. Interview with Joe Cassano.

131. "Downgrades and Downfall."

132. *The Financial Crisis Inquiry Report*, 334.

133. *The AIG Rescue, Its Impact on Markets, and the Government's Exit Strategy*.

134. *The AIG Rescue, Its Impact on Markets, and the Government's Exit Strategy*.

135. Dealbook, "H. Rodge Cohen: The Trauma Surgeon of Wall Street," *The New York Times*, November 15, 2009.

136. *The Financial Crisis Inquiry Report*, 344.

137. "Financial Crisis: Review of Federal Reserve System Financial Assistance to American International Group, Inc.," US Government Accountability Office, September 2011.

138. Stewart.

139. *The Financial Crisis Inquiry Report*, 142.

140. Stewart.

141. *The Financial Crisis Inquiry Report*, 61.

142. *The AIG Rescue, Its Impact on Markets, and the Government's Exit Strategy*, 49.

143. Stewart.

144. Stewart.

145. Stewart.

146. Stewart.

198. "President Obama Offers a Statement on the Attacks in Paris."

199. Donley, O'Leary, and Montgomery.

200. "November 2015 Paris Attacks."

201. Aaron David Miller, "Why the Paris Attacks Won't Be a Game-Changer for Obama," *Foreign Policy* (*FP*), November 18, 2015.

202. Jose Pagliery, "US Takes Aim at the ISIS Oil Business," CNN, December 11, 2015.

203. Domenico Montanaro, "US Political Reaction to Paris Attacks Split Along Party Lines," NPR, November 14, 2015.

204. Montanaro.

205. "November 2015 Paris Attacks."

206. Michael R. Gordon and Eric Schmitt, "US Steps Up Its Attacks on ISIS-Controlled Oil Fields in Syria," *The New York Times*, November 12, 2015.

207. Richard Sisk, "US Choice to Drop Leaflets in Syria Contrasts with Russian Way of War," Military.com, November 19, 2015.

208. Juliet Eilperin and Steven Mufson, "Recent Terrorist Attacks Push Obama to Reassess, and Defend, His Strategy," *The Washington Post*, December 7, 2015.

209. Miller.

210. Miller.

211. Miller.

212. Interview with Joe Cassano.

213. Morgenson.

214. Lewis.

215. Gautam Mukunda and Thomas J. DeLong, "Gerry Pasciucco at AIG Financial Products," *Harvard Business School Publishing*, July 31, 2013.

216. Robert O'Harrow Jr. and Brady Dennis, "The Beautiful Machine," *The Washington Post*, December 29, 2008.

217. "The Beautiful Machine."

218. "The Beautiful Machine."

219. Interview with Gary Gorton.

220. "The Beautiful Machine."

221. Interview with Maurice "Hank" Greenberg.

222. Interview with Andrew Forster.

223. Interview with Gene Park.

224. "A Crack in the System."

225. Mukunda and DeLong.

226. Interview with Joe Cassano.

227. Morgenson.

228. Lewis.

229. Interview with Joe Cassano. No charges were brought by either the US Department of Justice or the US Securities and Exchange Commission. They had determined that there was no basis for doing so. Cassano had not intended to cause harm. Rather, the system had failed. The *we* failed in allowing the subprime crisis to slowly bubble up in the shadow markets for several years prior to the crisis.

230. Lewis.

231. "Downgrades and Downfall."

232. Interview with Joe Cassano.

233. *The Financial Crisis Inquiry Report*, 213–227.

234. "A Crack in the System."

235. Interview with Gene Park.

236. Wikipedia, s.v. "Maurice R. Greenberg," accessed 2020, https://en.wikipedia.org/wiki/Maurice_R._Greenberg.

237. Jenny Anderson, "Greenberg and AIG Sever Ties," *The New York Times*, March 29, 2005.

238. "Hank Greenberg's Exit Marks the End of an Era," *Business Insurance*, March 20, 2005.

239. "Hank Greenberg's Exit Marks the End of an Era."

240. Monica Langley, "After a 37-Year Reign at AIG, Chief's Last Tumultuous Days," *The Wall Street Journal*, April 1, 2005.

241. Interview with Jon Liebergall.

242. Berger.

243. Anderson.

244. Anderson.

245. Carol J. Loomis, "AIG: Aggressive. Inscrutable. Greenberg.," *Fortune*, April 27, 1998.

246. Lewis.

247. Interview with Andrew Forster.

248. Morgenson.

249. Lewis.

250. Gautam and DeLong.

251. Loomis.

252. "Downgrades and Downfall."

253. Robert McDonald and Anna Paulson, *AIG in Hindsight*, Federal Reserve Bank of Chicago, October 2014.

254. *The Financial Crisis Inquiry Report*, 266.

255. *The Financial Crisis Inquiry Report*, 243.

256. Kandell.

257. Interview with Gary Gorton.

258. "Downgrades and Downfall."

259. Jake DeSantis, "Dear AIG, I Quit!," *The New York Times*, March 24, 2009.

260. Kandell.

261. Kandell.

262. Kandell.

263. Kandell.

264. Jeff Gerth, "In Private Papers, a More Candid Tim Geithner Speaks Out," *ProPublica*, October 30, 2014.

265. Carol D. Leonnig, "AIG Founder Wielded Personal Influence in Washington," *The Washington Post*, October 1, 2008.

266. *The Financial Crisis Inquiry Report*, 47–48.

267. Anthony Faiola, Ellen Nakashima, and Jill Drew, "What Went Wrong," *The Washington Post*, October 15, 2008.

268. *The Financial Crisis Inquiry Report*, xvii.

269. *The Financial Crisis Inquiry Report*, xxi.

270. Jackie Northam, "Hitting ISIS Where It Hurts by Striking Oil Trucks," NPR, November 19, 2015.

271. "Paris Terror Attacks: France Launches Fresh Airstrikes on ISIS in Syria—As It Happened."

272. Gordon and Schmitt.

273. Robert Burns, "US Says 116 Islamic State Oil Trucks Destroyed in Syria Airstrikes," TPM, November 17, 2015.

274. Sisk.

275. Northam.

276. Peter Baker and Eric Schmitt, "Paris Terror Attacks May Prompt More Aggressive US Strategy on ISIS," *The New York Times*, November 14, 2015.

277. "Paris Terror Attacks: France Launches Fresh Airstrikes on ISIS in Syria—As It Happened."

278. "Paris Terror Attacks: France Launches Fresh Airstrikes on ISIS in Syria—As It Happened."

279. Wikipedia, s.v. "November 2015 Paris Attacks."

280. Alissa J. Rubin and Anne Barnard, "France Strikes ISIS Targets in Syria in Retaliation for Attacks," *The New York Times*, November 15, 2015.

281. "Paris Terror Attacks: France Launches Fresh Airstrikes on ISIS in Syria—As It Happened."

282. *The AIG Rescue, Its Impact on Markets, and the Government's Exit Strategy*, 49.

283. *Financial Crisis Inquiry Report*, 334.

284. "The Attacks on Paris: Lessons Learned."

285. *Financial Crisis Inquiry Report*, 201.

286. Email from Gene Park to Joseph Cassano, "CDO of ABS Approach Going Forward—Message to the Dealer Community," February 28, 2006.

287. *Financial Crisis Inquiry Report*, 273.

288. Interview with Gary Gorton.

289. Interview with Joe Cassano.

290. Interview with Alan Frost.

291. "A Crack in the System."

292. In the fable, none of the men has encountered an elephant. Instead, they describe what they think the animal is based upon their perceptions from wherever they run their hands over the elephant: its trunk, its ear, its leg, its belly, or its tail. Their descriptions inevitably result in a grossly misshapen beast. Such distortion only increases through a game of telephone, in which the first person receives a message and then relays it to a second person, who in turn relays it to a third, and so on.

293. The George W. Bush Presidential Library and Museum centers on the exercise of judgment in crucible moments, including through interactive exhibits that allow visitors to experience rapidly changing situational contexts, fragmented fact patterns, and the need to make decisions under pressure. https://www.georgewbushlibrary.gov

294. "Downgrades and Downfall."

295. "The Beautiful Machine."

296. "A Crack in the System."

297. *Financial Crisis Inquiry Report*, 58.

298. Faiola, Nakashima, and Drew.

299. *Financial Crisis Inquiry Report*, 17.

300. Donadio.

301. Baker and Schmitt.

302. "Tactics, Techniques, and Procedures Used in the 13 November 2015 Paris Attacks," unclassified, *Joint Intelligence Bulletin*, November 23, 2015.

303. Stewart.

304. Stewart.

305. "Paris Terror Attacks: France Launches Fresh Airstrikes on ISIS in Syria—As It Happened."

306. *The AIG Rescue, Its Impact on Markets, and the Government's Exit Strategy*.

307. Interview with Joe Cassano.

308. Interview with Maurice "Hank" Greenberg.

309. Trent Elliott, "Complex Coordinated Terrorist Attack: Considerations for Practical Emergency Preparedness and Resiliency Exercises," *Wright State University*, 2017.

310. Elliott.

311. Berger.

312. *The Financial Crisis Inquiry Report*, 265.

313. Interview with Joe Cassano.

314. Stewart.

315. AIG compensated people extremely well. Much of this compensation, however, was deferred, whereby bonuses were reinvested in the company. Payout was deferred for five years, or in some cases, not until an executive retired from AIG. The purpose of the deferred compensation model was honorable. It was designed to ensure that decisions were made with a significant focus on the long-term health of AIG. The significant use of deferred compensation inextricably tied executives to the future of AIG. It forced peers to watch over their brethren to avoid mistakes, take on excess risk, or later be snapped by the long tail that extends from dumb decisions. However, when the US Department of the Treasury took over 79.9 percent of AIG's equity in conjunction with the bailout, these pools of deferred compensation were wiped out, along with the other shareholder equity. It was a blow. Executives started to get picked off by their competitors, including those financial institutions and hedge funds that had also participated in the development of the US subprime market and had been made whole by the terms of the government bailout. The AIG employees who remained thought they were continuing to be punished for the errors of a few.

316. Lewis.

Chris Mailander

Chris Mailander counsels corporate and national government clients through the arduous decision path faced in the pursuit of extraordinary outcomes. His client roster has included MasterCard, Bank of Montreal, the Federal Home Loan Bank System, Unisys, Visa, KPMG Consulting, BearingPoint, the President of Nigeria, the Government of Iraq, and a host of mid-market leaders and Silicon Valley innovators seeking to transform industries. He has negotiated tenders and commercial transactions in more than forty countries across North America, Europe, Asia, the Middle East, and Africa, including in conflict and post-conflict economies. He was previously an adjunct professor at Georgetown University Law School and an adjunct fellow at the Center for Strategic & International Studies. He lives in Asheville, North Carolina.